Shakespeare on the Double!™

The Taming of the Shrew

Shakespeare on the Double!™

The Taming of the Shrew

translated by

Mary Ellen Snodgrass

Wiley Publishing, Inc.

Published by Wiley Publishing, Inc., Hoboken, New Jersey

For general information on our other products and services or to obtain technical support please contact our Customer Care Department within the U.S. at (800) 762-2974, outside the U.S. at (317) 572-3993 or fax (317) 572-4002.

Wiley also publishes its books in a variety of electronic formats. Some content that appears in print may not be available in electronic books. For more information about Wiley products, please visit our web site at www.wiley.com.

Library of Congress Cataloging-in-Publication data is available from the publisher upon request.

ISBN: 978-0-470-21276-9

Printed in the United States of America

10 9 8 7 6 5 4 3 2 1

Book design by Melissa Auciello-Brogan
Book production by Wiley Publishing, Inc. Composition Services

Contents

About the Translator

Mary Ellen Snodgrass is an award-winning author of textbooks and general reference works and a former columnist for the *Charlotte Observer.* A member of Phi Beta Kappa, she graduated magna cum laude from the University of North Carolina at Greensboro and Appalachian State University and holds degrees in English, Latin, psychology, and education of gifted children.

Introduction

Shakespeare on the Double! The Taming of the Shrew provides the full text of the Bard's play side by side with an easy-to-read modern English translation that you can understand. You no longer have to struggle wondering what exactly "Our purses shall be proud" means! You can read the Shakespearean text on the left-hand pages and check the right-hand pages when Shakespeare's language stumps you. Or you can read only the translation, which enables you to understand the action and characters without struggling through the Shakespearean English. You can even read both, referring back and forth easily between the original text and the modern translation. Any way you choose, you can now fully understand every line of the Bard's masterpiece!

We've also provided you with some additional resources:

- **Brief synopsis** of the plot and action offers a broad-strokes overview of the play.
- **Comprehensive character list** covers the actions, motivations, and characteristics of each major player.
- **Visual character map** displays who the major characters are and how they relate to one another.
- **Cycle of love** pinpoints the sequence of love in the play, including who *truly* loves whom, and who *mistakenly* loves whom.
- **Reflective questions** help you delve even more into the themes and meanings of the play.

Reading Shakespeare can be slow and difficult. No more! With *Shakespeare on the Double! The Taming of the Shrew,* you can read the play in language that you can grasp quickly and thoroughly.

Synopsis

INDUCTION

Scene 1

A maid at a barroom on a heath tosses out Christopher Sly, a drunken beggar. Sly sinks into sleep. When a lord returns from hunting with dogs, he devises a plan to have his household convince Sly that he is a lord recovering from seven years of insanity. Servants carry Sly to the finest bedroom, offer him delicacies and water for washing, and dress him in fine clothes to convince him that he owns the lavish mansion. While Sly sleeps off his binge, an acting troupe arrives. They conspire with the lord to dupe Sly. The lord requests the performance of a comedy later that evening. The lord assigns his servant Bartholomew to disguise himself as Sly's wife.

Scene 2

Christopher Sly awakens in a lovely bedchamber in a strange house with attendants ready to wait on him. Bewildered, Sly calls for a mug of beer. The servants pretend to be overjoyed that their master has recovered after having been delusional the past fifteen years. They make up tales of all the harsh dreams of poverty brought about by his madness and convince him that he is lord of the estate. He invites his wife to come to bed with him. Bartholomew declares that the doctor forbids sex, which might cause a relapse. The players agree to entertain the group with a comedy. Sly, Bartholomew, and the household settle in for the performance.

ACT I

Scene 1

With the servant Tranio, Lucentio, a Pisan traveler and son of the wealthy merchant Vincentio, arrives at a street before the house of Baptista in Padua. Reared in Florence, Lucentio intends to rent quarters and to enroll at the University of Padua. Tranio encourages his master to sample philosophy and any subject that pleases him but doesn't turn him into a bore. Lucentio and Tranio eavesdrop as Baptista Minola, a rich gentleman of Padua, approaches with his two daughters, the fractious Katherina and her amiable younger sister Bianca. Accompanying them are the elderly neighbor Gremio and the foolish Hortensio, two suitors for Bianca.

Baptista ends the men's courtship of Bianca because Katherina must wed before her younger sister. Kate is a sharp-tongued scold. Because of her reputation for squabbling, Hortensio and Gremio doubt that she will ever marry. Hortensio charges Baptista with being cruel to Bianca, the younger, more agreeable and desirable daughter. Baptista sends Bianca indoors to study music and poetry. He asks if the suitors can recommend tutors for his girls. Both suitors agree to find Katherina a husband so that they may compete for Bianca.

Lucentio is infatuated with Bianca at first sight. Tranio proposes that Lucentio disguise himself as a schoolmaster to be nearer Bianca. The servant reminds his master that he is expected in Padua. As a remedy, Lucentio tells Tranio to impersonate him while Lucentio disguises himself as a tutor. Because no one in Padua knows either man, the two exchange clothes and identities. Lucentio's servant Biondello arrives and is confused to see Tranio wearing his master's garments. Lucentio lies to Biondello that Tranio has agreed to impersonate him because Lucentio killed a man on the shore in Padua and fears retaliation.

The audience interrupts after Sly dozes off. Bartholomew, disguised as Sly's wife, admires the comedy. Christopher hopes that it ends soon.

Scene 2

Petruchio and his servant Grumio from Verona arrive in Padua to visit acquaintances. Petruchio knocks at his old friend Hortensio's house and describes his home and financial situation since the death of his father Antonio. Hortensio jokingly asks Petruchio whether he would like a rich, harsh-tongued wife. Petruchio asserts that no nag could be so shrewish, so unattractive, or so wayward, as long as her dowry was sufficient. He swears to wed Katherina Minola, daughter of Antonio's old friend. Grumio adds that Petruchio has the charm and persistence to overpower a shrew.

Hortensio volunteers to accompany Petruchio to Baptista's house, where Bianca is confined. Since Bianca's father refuses to let her have suitors, Hortensio asks Petruchio to identify him in disguise as Litio, a music tutor. Gremio arrives with Lucentio, who wears the disguise of the schoolmaster Cambio. In offering Lucentio as a tutor to Baptista's daughters, Gremio instructs the Pisan scholar to court Bianca on Gremio's behalf by reading romance to her.

When all the visitors meet, Hortensio informs Gremio that he, too, has found a tutor for Bianca. Hortensio also states he has also found a man who wants to marry Kate to obtain her dowry. Petruchio, undaunted by Gremio's warnings of Kate's foul temper, assures the men that he has a way with balky wildcats. Tranio, disguised as Lucentio, appears with Biondello on the way to the house of Baptista, a family friend. Tranio tells Gremio and Hortensio that he, too, shall be considered as a suitor for Bianca. Tranio wishes Petruchio well in courting the spiteful older sister Kate and invites the men for a drink.

ACT II

Scene 1

At the Minola house, Katherina ties Bianca's hands. Kate drags her sister behind her and demands to know which suitor Bianca loves. Bianca, a bit frightened by her sister's actions, offers to give Kate her jewelry and clothes in exchange for freedom. Bianca claims to love no suitor and offers Kate either Hortensio or the wealthy Gremio. Baptista intercedes for Bianca, who weeps. After untying her and sending her to do needlework, he scolds Kate for being an unruly daughter. She accuses him of preferring Bianca and of marrying off Kate, even if the betrothal humiliates her.

Gremio, Lucentio disguised as Cambio, Petruchio, Hortensio disguised as Litio, Tranio disguised as Lucentio, and Biondello enter the Minola house. Petruchio announces his interest in courting Kate and presents Hortensio disguised as Litio as a math and music tutor to the two daughters. Baptista welcomes Petruchio, but admits that the newcomer is mistaken in his impression of Kate's disposition. Seeing Baptista's easy acceptance of Litio's services, Gremio quickly advances Lucentio disguised as Cambio, as a scholar trained at Rheims, France, in math, music, the classics, and other languages. Baptista welcomes Cambio. Tranio introduces himself as a Pisan, Vincentio's son, and a suitor for Bianca. He brings as gifts a lute and some Greek and Latin books. Baptista sends the tutors to his daughters.

Petruchio moves rapidly to the question of Kate's dowry, which is half Baptista's property plus ten thousand dollars payable immediately to the potential groom. Petruchio wants to draw up the marriage contract, but Baptista insists the suitor must first win Kate's love. As Petruchio and Baptista discuss Petruchio's hearty style of wooing, Hortensio disguised as Litio returns with a broken lute, which Kate smashed over his head. Baptista sends the wary tutor to train Bianca.

The details of Kate's insults to Hortensio whet Petruchio's interest. When Petruchio and Kate meet, he insists that she is a demure, lovely woman. She disdains his romantic blather. They banter and exchange quips until she slaps him. He threatens to strike her back. She questions his honor. Petruchio vows to marry her despite her obvious objections.

When the men return, Kate accuses Baptista of betrothing her to a halfwit. Gremio fears that he has no chance of courting Bianca. Petruchio sets the wedding for Sunday and declares to Gremio that Kate is gentler in private. Baptista shakes hands on the match. Petruchio departs to buy wedding necessities in Venice.

Gremio and Tranio disguised as Vincentio vie for Bianca by listing for Baptista all the wealth they can offer her. Whatever Gremio pledges, Tranio offers more. Baptista approves Tranio's dower, which includes seventeen ships. Although Gremio accepts defeat, Tranio's father must prove that the offer is real. In private, Gremio accuses Tranio of bluffing. Tranio now realizes that, to win Bianca for his master, he must find an impersonator of Vincentio. If Tranio fails, Gremio will marry Bianca.

ACT III

Scene 1

In the classrooom, Lucentio disguised as the Latin teacher Cambio and Hortensio disguised as the musician Litio compete for Bianca's affection. They quarrel over who should begin Bianca's lessons. She refuses to be treated like a child and resolves the dispute. She orders Hortensio to tune his lute while she studies Latin with Lucentio.

While pretending to translate a Latin text about the setting of the Trojan War, Lucentio confesses his true identity and his love for Bianca. She gently rebukes him, but doesn't reject him. When Hortensio gets his chance to teach Bianca, she humors him while he introduces a fake musical scale. When Bianca leaves to decorate Kate's room for the wedding, Lucentio accompanies her. Hortensio begins to realize Cambio is romancing Bianca. He vows that if Bianca proves fickle, he will get even by courting another woman.

Scene 2

On Sunday morning, all except Petruchio await the nuptials. As the wedding party anticipates the tardy groom, Kate refuses to be humiliated publicly and leaves. Baptista sides with his weeping daughter. Tranio asserts that Petruchio is dependable. Biondello announces that Petruchio is on his way dressed in worn, mismatched clothes and riding an old, diseased horse. Grumio travels along in similarly disgraceful attire. When Petruchio rides in, he refuses to change into clothing that Tranio offers. Petruchio explains that Kate will wed him, not his clothes.

The wedding party advances to the church, where Petruchio plans to kiss his bride at the altar. Lucentio and Tranio discuss their need of an impostor to play the role of Vincentio. Gremio returns with a description of an outrageous and profane wedding. Petruchio swore during the ceremony and knocked the priest to the floor. The ceremony concluded with a loud smooch and with Petruchio downing the ritual wine. The groom's behavior was so unthinkable that Gremio was embarrassed.

At the reception, Petruchio declares the wedding feast shall take place but that the bride and groom must leave before sundown. Kate, furious at missing the celebration, insists on staying, but Petruchio refuses. Gremio reveals that the stubborn bride is the real Kate. She asserts that obedient wives get what they deserve. While Grumio draws his sword, Petruchio claims his wife and departs from guests he charges with wanting to kidnap the bride. Bianca thinks the volatile pair suited to each other. Baptista invites the wedding guests to dine and places Bianca and Lucentio at the head of the table in place of the real bride and groom.

ACT IV

Scene 1

At Petruchio's country house, the staff—Nathaniel, Joseph, Nicholas, Phillip, Walter, Sugarsop, Gabriel, Peter, Walter, Adam, Rafe, Gregory, Curtis, and the rest—cleans and prepares the hall as the newlyweds approach. Through the rain, Grumio precedes them over muddy roads to build a fire. He tells Curtis that Kate and Petruchio have fought the entire way. At one point, Katherina's horse stumbled and fell on her. Petruchio ignores his bride and beats Grumio for the mishap. Katherina, covered in mud, wades through the mire and pulls Petruchio off Grumio. The harness breaks, and the horses escape.

When Kate and Petruchio arrive, Grumio spruces up the servants to greet the newlyweds. Petruchio rants at his serving men for not meeting him at the door to take charge of his horse. The couple proceeds to dinner. As Kate's washes, a serving man earns a scolding for accidentally dropping the pitcher. Kate defends the servant for the mishap. When dinner arrives, Petruchio criticizes the burned meat and throws the food and dishes at the staff. He claims to protect Kate from food that arouses anger. Choosing an evening's fast, Petruchio leads Kate to the bedroom and continues lecturing her. In private, Petruchio explains his intent to keep Kate hungry and sleepless until he tames her.

Scene 2

Tranio asks Hortensio if Bianca is interested in Cambio. Tranio and Hortensio spy on Cambio's lessons from the *Art of Love*. The couple concludes with kissing and caressing. The spies ponder the inconstancy of women. Hortensio reveals his true identity to Tranio, who agrees to reject Bianca. Hortensio plans to marry a wealthy widow in three days. Lucentio, Bianca, and Tranio are pleased to hear Hortensio has abandoned his pursuit of Bianca. Tranio claims that Hortensio gained a new attitude toward difficult women by studying Petruchio's methods.

Biondello reports the arrival of an old Mantuan, either a peddler or a scholar. The man claims to travel south to Rome and north to Tripoli, Italy. Tranio entices the old man to pose as Vincentio. Tranio makes up a death sentence in Padua against Mantuans because of enmity between the Duke of Padua and the Duke of Mantua. Tranio agrees to change Florentine coins for the old man if the newcomer disguises himself as Vincentio of Pisa and hides in Lucentio's house. In return, the old man must confirm the dowry that Lucentio offered Baptista for Bianca.

Scene 3

At Petruchio's country house, Kate orders Grumio to bring her some nourishment. Grumio taunts Kate with a menu of meats, but he overrules each dish as bad for her disposition. Kate pummels Grumio for tormenting her with visions of food. When Petruchio and Hortensio enter, the groom offers Kate meat that he cuts for her. Until she thanks him, he withholds it. She receives the plate after meekly thanking him. He urges Hortensio in private to eat the meat.

Petruchio announces that the household will dress in fine clothes and return to Baptista's house. Petruchio confers with a tailor presenting a gown and a haberdasher offering a cap, both for Kate. The groom belittles the cap, even though Kate likes it. He then faults the gown. Grumio attests that the tailor didn't follow the master's directions. In secret, Petruchio arranges to pay the tailor the next day. Petruchio declares their old clothes suitable for the journey. When he claims it is currently 7 a.m., Kate states that it is almost 2 p.m., too late to reach Padua by noon. Petruchio postpones the trip until Kate stops contradicting him.

Scene 4

Tranio disguised as Lucentio and the scholar disguised as Lucentio's father Vincentio confer with Baptista Minola about the dowry. When the scholar attests to the love match, he eloquently confirms to Baptista the dowry's availability. Tranio suggests that the two men draw up the contract. Baptista wants to complete the signing far from Gremio's view. Tranio offers his quarters and sends for a notary. The host apologizes for his lack of suitable refreshments.

Baptista sends Cambio to tell Bianca the success of the nuptial negotiation. Biondello informs Lucentio of Tranio's plan to arrange a fake wedding with a fake groom and a fake father-in-law. Meanwhile, a priest waits at St. Luke's church to wed Lucentio to Bianca. Lucentio hurries off to escort Bianca to the church. Biondello follows to ensure success.

Scene 5

At noon, Petruchio, Kate, and Hortensio travel from the country to Baptista Minola's house in Padua. Petruchio notes the moon shines brightly. Because of Kate's contradiction that the sun is shining, Petruchio threatens to return home. Kate realizes that she must humor him to get what she wants. She agrees with whatever Petruchio says. When Vincentio, father to Lucentio, meets the travelers, Petruchio tests Kate by identifying Vincentio as a lovely maiden.

Once the couple halts their test of marital dominance, Vincentio explains that he is traveling from Pisa to visit his son in Padua. Petruchio introduces himself as Lucentio's new brother-in-law. Vincentio is stunned to discover that Lucentio has married Bianca Minola. The party moves on toward Padua, leaving Hortensio marveling at the change in Kate's stubbornness. He plans to follow Petruchio's example and tame the widow.

ACT V

Scene 1

Lucentio and Bianca hurry to their wedding while her father negotiates with Tranio and the scholar. Petruchio, Kate, Vincentio, and Grumio arrive in Padua and stop at Lucentio's house. Vincentio insists his companions join him for a drink. Upon knocking, he discovers a man at the window who claims to be the father of Lucentio, who is too busy to come to the door. When Biondello returns from the wedding, Vincentio questions him.

Biondello pretends not to recognize his old master. Petruchio vouches for Vincentio, who fears identity theft.

Vincentio threatens Biondello. Petruchio and Kate pause to watch the commotion. When Tranio comes to investigate, he too pretends not to know Vincentio. The old man mourns the waste of money on Tranio's fine clothes. When the scholar defends Tranio disguised as Lucentio, Vincentio identifies Tranio as the son of a sailmaker in Bergamo. Vincentio reared Tranio from age three. Tranio summons an officer of the watch. The old man fears that Tranio murdered his young master and assumed his persona. Gremio believes Vincentio's story. Baptista orders Vincentio's arrest and jailing.

When Lucentio and Bianca return from their wedding, the groom ignores Biondello's warning and kneels before Vincentio to ask forgiveness. Bianca asks pardon of her father for eloping. Lucentio explains why Tranio was masquerading as his master. Gremio, realizing he has lost Bianca, anticipates a meal at the wedding feast. Petruchio and Kate continue to eavesdrop on the uproar. He demands a public kiss, which she disapproves of, but allows.

Scene 2

At Lucentio's house, guests celebrate Bianca and Lucentio's wedding with formal welcomes to the two fathers. Hortensio escorts his new wife, the Widow, to the reception. Petruchio notes how Hortensio appears to be afraid of his wife; the widow retorts that Petruchio believes all husbands are like himself. Kate demands an explanation. The widow insults Kate as a nag. Bianca inserts an insult and escorts the women to the parlor.

The husbands bet on whose wife is most obedient. Petruchio, confident in Kate's moderation, raises the stakes. They wager one hundred crowns and one by one send for their wives. Bianca ignores Lucentio's summons. The widow refuses the call and tells Hortensio to come to her. To Petruchio's command, Kate comes immediately. Petruchio sends Kate to fetch the other women and tells her to stamp on the cap she wears. After discarding her cap, she lectures the wives on marital duty. After Kate delivers an elaborate speech about a woman's duty to her husband, Petruchio and Kate go to bed. Hortensio and Lucentio ponder Petruchio's power over his wife.

List of Characters

Christopher Sly A gullible, but proud tinker in the Induction. After passing out drunk at a pub, he finds himself living a poor man's dream—sleeping in a fine house and decked in jewelry and rich clothes. Sly falls for a trick that elevates him to a married aristocrat. He believes he is recovering from fifteen years of mental illness that reduced him to beggary for seven years.

A lord A rural gentleman in the Induction. He boasts of quality hunting hounds. For amusement, he deceives Christopher Sly into living like a privileged country squire.

Bartholomew The lord's page. Dressed in women's clothes, Bartholomew plays the soft-spoken beauty who is wed to Christopher Sly, but who denies him sex. The pose introduces the theme of female compliance to her husband.

Servants, huntsmen The lord's staff and companions. They overwhelm Christopher Sly with personal service befitting a nobleman.

Players A troupe of actors in the Induction. When they happen to arrive at the pub, they amuse the lord by coddling Christopher Sly.

Hostess A pub waitress who threatens Christopher Sly for refusing to pay for breaking glasses. By threatening to summon the sheriff, she introduces the motif of the formidable female.

Baptista Minola A genteel Paduan and father of Bianca and Katherina. He congratulates himself for generosity by hiring tutors for his daughters and by offering Katherina's suitor 20,000 crowns. According to tradition, Baptista insists that his older daughter marry Petruchio on Sunday before the younger one is wed the following week. In choosing among suitors of Bianca, he offers her to Tranio/Lucentio, the man who promises the most money. Baptista's mercenary attitude toward daughters illustrates gender bias toward women as objects to sell like livestock. He redeems himself somewhat by sharing Katherina's embarrassment that Petruchio comes late to the wedding. Ironically, both daughters manipulate and outfox their father.

Katherina Minola/Kate An aggressive, sharp-tongued heiress who believes that women must fight for their rights. She refuses her father's attempts to entrap her in a hasty marriage. She pictures herself as a spinster to be humiliated by Bianca's wedding. To build self-esteem, Katherina develops a bristly exterior and counters her father's preference for his appealing younger daughter, the family pet. By dropping her guard, Katherina finds love with an equally hard-edged suitor and fears being abased by his failure to arrive on time to their wedding. She takes a pragmatic course in wedlock by agreeing with whatever Petruchio says.

Bianca Minola A deceptively demure, compliant daughter who reads poetry, does needlework, and plays the lute. Bianca cloaks a competitive nature and makes her own schedules for lessons and wooing. She agrees to elope with her beau Lucentio, who believes her to be obedient and serious. In the falling action, Bianca appears to swap natures with Katherina, who has evolved into a submissive and loving wife while Bianca displays a stubborn streak.

Petruchio A jaunty aristocrat, war veteran, and boisterous fortune hunter from Verona. After his father Antonio's death leaves him property and money, Petruchio visits Hortensio in Padua before looking for a bride. On Hortensio's advice, Petruchio tracks down a loud-mouthed heiress, Katherina Minola, as a potential wife. Before meeting her, he divulges his own nature by preferring a challenge—a scrappy female who demands domestication into the traditional role of subservient mate. By breaching wedding courtesies, he mimics her violation of refined womanhood and concludes the ceremony with a comic version of bride capture.

Hortensio/Litio A limp, unappealing suitor. Disguised as Litio of Mantua, a music and math teacher, he is easily victimized by Katherina, who whacks him with a lute. To his rival, he offers fair competition for Bianca and her dowry and proposes making her available for courtship by finding a husband for Katherina. After studying Petruchio's methods of wife taming, Hortensio adopts the controlling attitude of a jealous mate. Upon losing his quest, three days later, he marries a widow who appears as stubborn as her rival.

Lucentio/Cambio The handsome only son of the wealthy Vincentio. Lucentio travels from Pisa to Lombardy to study, but falls in love at first sight of Bianca Minola's tender loveliness. Disguised as the commoner Cambio, a teacher educated at Rheims in math, music, classics, and other languages, Lucentio plots to gain access to her by reading philosophy aloud. He creates comic relief by translating a Latin epic as though it were a love message. With Tranio's help, Lucentio proposes outwitting Gremio by eloping with Bianca. Shortly after marriage, Lucentio displays the courtesies of a contented squire and host to his father-in-law.

Gremio An aged suitor and a quitter at romance. Gremio, who is too weak to control a woman as shrill as Katherina, is rival to Hortensio for Bianca Minola. He accentuates his servility to Baptista by groveling and bargaining with a richly appointed house. Baptista suspects Gremio of eavesdropping.

Grumio A foolish serving man and the brunt of Petruchio's impatience. Grumio plays dumb while attempting to please his master. During the taming of Katherina, Grumio is a willing accomplice in depriving her of food.

Biondello Lucentio's serving man, who is leery of disguised identities. Biondello poses as his master and carries a lute and classical texts to Bianca. He serves the play as an eyewitness to Petruchio's absurd behavior on the way to the church and during the wedding. Biondello also works out details of Lucentio's elopement with Bianca.

Tranio/Lucentio Lucentio's serving man whom Vincentio reared from age three. Tranio is a proponent of a liberal education, but a skeptic of love at first sight. A facile liar, he trades roles with his master and manipulates Baptista by pretending to be an expert on classical literature. Tranio's wooing of Bianca involves an accounting of Lucentio's inherited wealth, which includes 17 ships. In a second role shift, Tranio poses as Vincentio, Lucentio's father, and furthers the elopement plot.

Vincentio A wealthy Pisan merchant and father of Lucentio. Vincentio demands order by instructing Tranio to be a good servant. A disgruntled squire, Vincentio finds nothing amusing about his son's trading of positions with a servant and wasting money on fine clothes for Tranio.

A widow A lusty individualist. Like Katherina Minola, the widow marries a controlling male, Hortensio, but proves him ineffective in subduing her and taming her tongue.

pedant/Vincentio An itinerant Mantuan teacher. On his way to Rome and Tripoli, he poses temporarily as Vincentio to aid Lucentio's wooing of Bianca.

Curtis Petruchio's houseboy. To Grumio's blatherings, Curtis seeks news from Padua. To complete homecoming preparations, he summons **Nathaniel, Joseph, Nicholas, Phillip, Walter, Sugarsop,** and the rest of the house staff.

Character Map

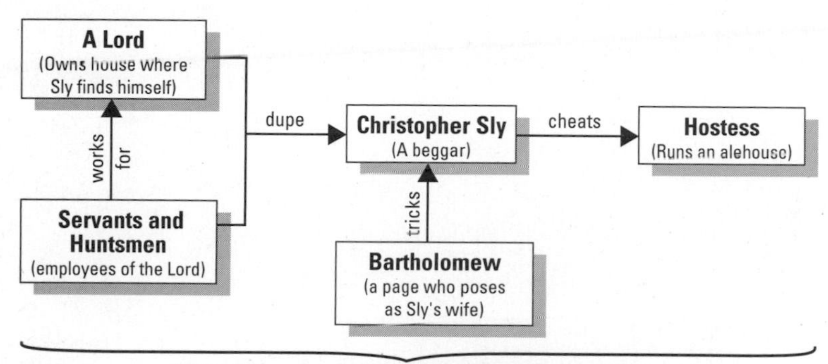

All watch a play featuring the following players:

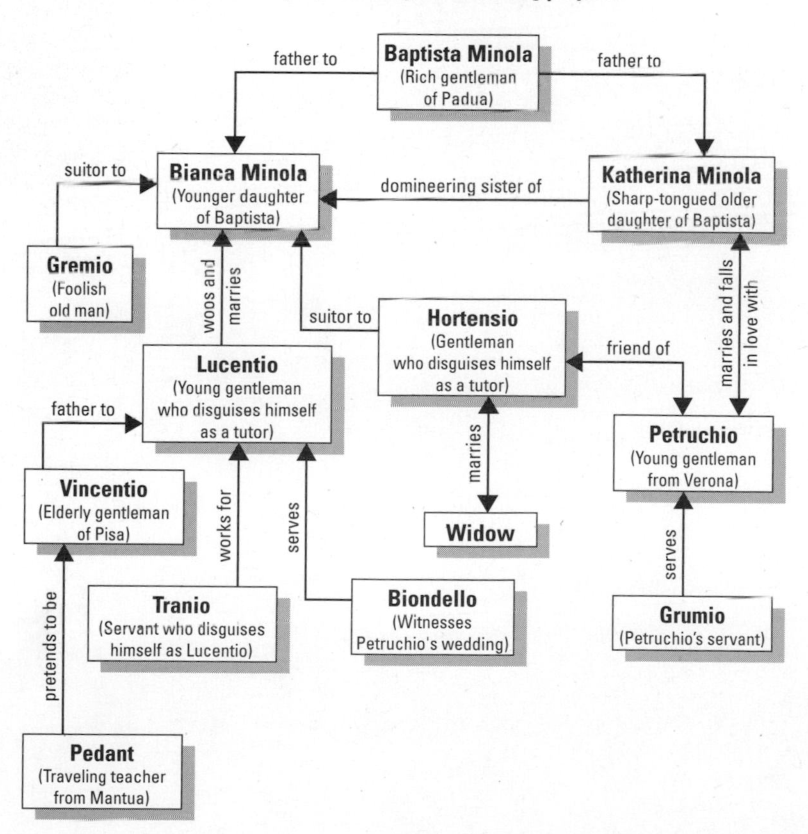

Cycle of Love

To thwart a domineering father, Kate maneuvers against a wily suitor. The graphic below describes the multiple ruses that unite Kate with Petruchio and free Kate's sister Bianca to marry her beau.

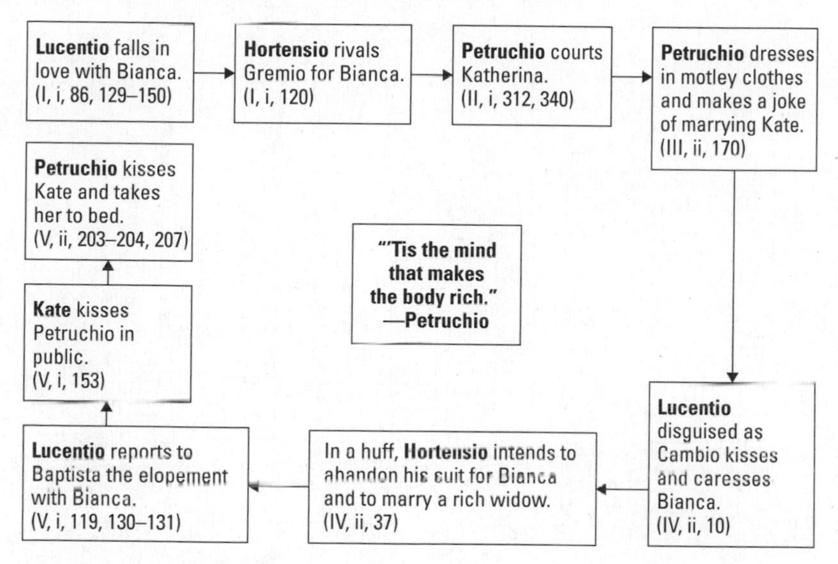

Shakespeare's
The Taming of the Shrew

INDUCTION, SCENE 1

Before an alehouse on a heath.

[Enter CHRISTOPHER SLY and the HOSTESS]

SLY I'll feeze you, in faith.

HOSTESS A pair of stocks, you rogue!

SLY Y'are a baggage, the Slys are no rogues. Look in the
Chronicles. We came in with Richard Conqueror.
Therefore, pocas palabras, let the world slide. Sessa! 5

HOSTESS You will not pay for the glasses you have burst?

SLY No, not a denier. Go by, Saint Jeronimy! Go to thy cold
bed and warm thee.

HOSTESS I know my remedy. I must go fetch the third-borough.
[Exit]

SLY Third, or fourth, or fifth borough, I'll answer him by law. 10
I'll not budge an inch, boy. Let him come, and kindly.
[Lies down on the ground, and falls asleep]
[Wind horns. Enter a LORD from hunting, with his TRAIN]

LORD Huntsman, I charge thee, tender well my hounds.
Breathe Merriman (the poor cur is emboss'd)
And couple Clowder with the deep-mouth'd brach.
Saw'st thou not, boy, how Silver made it good 15
At the hedge-corner, in the coldest fault?
I would not lose the dog for twenty pound.

FIRST HUNTSMAN Why, Bellman is as good as he, my lord.
He cried upon it at the merest loss,
And twice to-day pick'd out the dullest scent. 20
Trust me, I take him for the better dog.

LORD Thou art a fool. If Echo were as fleet,
I would esteem him worth a dozen such.
But sup them well, and look unto them all.
To-morrow I intend to hunt again. 25

FIRST HUNTSMAN I will, my lord.

INDUCTION, SCENE 1

Introduction to the Comedy
In front of a barroom on an open stretch of shrubby land.

[The alehouse barmaid and the beggar CHRISTOPER SLY enter.]

SLY I swear, I'll fix you.

HOSTESS You'll go to the pillory, you rascal!

SLY You are a saucy woman. The Sly family are all respectable. Check British history. We arrived in 1066 with Richard the Conqueror, the invader from Normandy. So, say no more. So much for the world's criticism. That's enough!

HOSTESS You won't reimburse me for the glasses you've broken?

SLY No, not a portion of a penny. Out with you, Saint Jerome. Go to bed and get warm.

HOSTESS I know how to stop you. I'll go for the sheriff. *[The hostess exits the barroom.]*

SLY Go to the third, fourth, or fifth county sheriff. I can defend myself against the law. I'm not moving from this bar. Let the sheriff come and welcome. *[CHRISTOPHER SLY falls asleep at the bar.] [Hunters blow their horns. A lord enters the bar with his hunting party.]*

LORD Hunting master, take care of my dog pack. Rest Merriman. The poor hound is exhausted. Pair Clowder with the deep-voiced bitch. Did you notice, boy, how silver found our quarry at the hedge corner where the scent was faintest? I wouldn't give up Silver for forty dollars.

FIRST HUNTSMAN Bellman is as good a hunter as Silver, my lord. He bayed the quarry when the scent was faintest. Twice today he followed the weakest trail. In my opinion, Bellman is a better hunter than Silver.

LORD You are wrong. If Echo were as fast, I would claim him more valuable than a dozen like Bellman. Feed them well and tend to them. I want to hunt with them again tomorrow.

FIRST HUNTSMAN I will, my lord.

LORD *[Sees SLY]* What's here? One dead, or drunk?
See, doth he breathe?

SECOND HUNTSMAN He breathes, my lord. Were he not warm'd with ale,
This were a bed but cold to sleep so soundly. 30

LORD O monstrous beast! How like a swine he lies!
Grim death, how foul and loathsome is thine image!
Sirs, I will practise on this drunken man.
What think you, if he were convey'd to bed,
Wrapp'd in sweet clothes, rings put upon his fingers, 35
A most delicious banquet by his bed,
And brave attendants near him when he wakes.
Would not the beggar then forget himself?

FIRST HUNTSMAN Believe me, lord, I think he cannot choose.

SECOND HUNTSMAN It would seem strange unto him when he wak'd. 40

LORD Even as a flattering dream or worthless fancy.
Then take him up, and manage well the jest.
Carry him gently to my fairest chamber,
And hang it round with all my wanton pictures.
Balm his foul head in warm distillèd waters, 45
And burn sweet wood to make the lodging sweet.
Procure me music ready when he wakes,
To make a dulcet and a heavenly sound.
And if he chance to speak, be ready straight
And, with a low, submissive reverence, 50
Say 'What is it your honour will command?'
Let one attend him with a silver basin
Full of rose-water and bestrew'd with flowers,
Another bear the ewer, the third a diaper,
And say 'Will't please your lordship cool your hands?' 55
Some one be ready with a costly suit,
And ask him what apparel he will wear.
Another tell him of his hounds and horse,
And that his lady mourns at his disease.
Persuade him that he hath been lunatic, 60
And, when he says he is, say that he dreams,
For he is nothing but a mighty lord.
This do, and do it kindly, gentle sirs.
It will be pastime passing excellent,
If it be husbanded with modesty. 65

LORD *[Sees SLY]* Who's this? Is he dead or drunk? Check his breathing.

SECOND HUNTSMAN He's alive, my lord. If beer didn't keep him warm, he wouldn't sleep so soundly in a cold bed.

LORD What an animal! He lies at the bar like a pig! He looks as grim and grotesque as death! Gentlemen, I will play a trick on this drunkard. We could carry him to bed, dress him in comfy clothes, and put rings on his fingers. We could place a feast by his bed and servants near him when he wakes up. Might he forget that he is a beggar?

FIRST HUNTSMAN I doubt that he has a choice about being a pauper, my lord.

SECOND HUNTSMAN He would be amazed when he woke up.

LORD He will think he is dreaming or is lost in fantasy. Pick him up and carry out the trick. Move him easy to my best bedroom. Hang sexy pictures on the wall. Bathe his dirty face with warm water. Burn fragrant wood on the hearth to make the room pleasant. Have musicians ready when he rouses to produce a sweet, heavenly sound. If he talks to you, reply with a low, humble bow. Say, "What would your honor like?" Let one of you offer him a silver bowl of rosewater sprinkled with blossoms. Another present the pitcher; the third man, a hand towel. Say, "Would it please your lordship to rinse your hands?" Someone offer an expensive outfit. Ask what clothing he wants to wear. Remark on his dogs and horse. Say that his wife is sorry he is sick. Convince him that he has been insane. When he agrees with you, say that he is dreaming. Convince him he is a powerful lord. Do all this realistically, kind gentlemen. It will be fun If you restrain your laughter.

FIRST HUNTSMAN My lord, I warrant you we will play our part
As he shall think by our true diligence
He is no less than what we say he is.

LORD Take him up gently, and to bed with him,
And each one to his office when he wakes. 70
[SLY is carried off; sound trumpets]
Sirrah, go see what trumpet 'tis that sounds.
[Exit SERVINGMAN]
Belike some noble gentleman that means,
Travelling some journey, to repose him here.
[Enter SERVINGMAN]
How now! Who is it?

SERVANT An't please your Honour, players 75
That offer service to your lordship.

LORD Bid them come near.
[Enter PLAYERS]
Now, fellows, you are welcome.

PLAYERS We thank your Honour.

LORD Do you intend to stay with me tonight? 80

FIRST PLAYER So please your Lordship to accept our duty.

LORD With all my heart. This fellow I remember
Since once he play'd a farmer's eldest son.
'Twas where you woo'd the gentlewoman so well.
I have forgot your name, but, sure, that part 85
Was aptly fitted and naturally perform'd.

SECOND PLAYER I think 'twas Soto that your Honour means.

LORD 'Tis very true; thou didst it excellent.
Well, you are come to me in happy time,
The rather for I have some sport in hand 90
Wherein your cunning can assist me much.
There is a lord will hear you play tonight;
But I am doubtful of your modesties,
Lest, over-eying of his odd behaviour
For yet his Honour never heard a play, 95
You break into some merry passion
And so offend him. For I tell you, sirs,
If you should smile, he grows impatient.

FIRST PLAYER Fear not, my lord, we can contain ourselves
Were he the veriest antick in the world. 100

FIRST HUNTSMAN	I guarantee, my lord, that we will act our parts well. Our efforts will convince him that he is what we say he is.
LORD	Carry him upstairs gently and put him to bed. Do your parts when he wakes up. *[Some men carry CHRISTOPHER SLY to bed. A hunting trumpet sounds.]* Servant, see who is blowing the hunting horn. *[A servant departs.]* Perhaps a nobleman is traveling here to spend the night. *[The servant returns.]* Well, who is it?
SERVANT	An acting troupe has arrived to perform for you.
LORD	Invite them in. *[The acting company enters the barroom.]* Players, I welcome you.
PLAYERS	We are grateful, sir.
LORD	Do you intend to remain here tonight?
FIRST PLAYER	If you want us to stay.
LORD	Truly, I do. I remember this actor from the time that he played a farmer's eldest son. You courted a lady well. I've forgotten your name. But I remember how well suited you were for the role and how well you played it.
SECOND PLAYER	You refer to the character Soto.
LORD	That was his name. You played him well. You have come at the perfect time. I am playing a trick that you may help me with. A lord will watch you perform tonight. I doubt you can control your laughter. Don't stare at his peculiar behavior. He has never been to a play. If you all laugh, you will insult him. I promise, if you even smile, he will be annoyed.
FIRST PLAYER	Don't worry, my lord. We can control ourselves, even if he were the craziest man in the world.

LORD *[to a SERVINGMAN]* Go, sirrah, take them to the buttery
And give them friendly welcome every one.
Let them want nothing that my house affords.
[Exit one with the PLAYERS]
[to another servingman] Sirrah, go you to Barthol'mew my page,
And see him dress'd in all suits like a lady. 105
That done, conduct him to the drunkard's chamber,
And call him 'madam,' do him obeisance.
Tell him from me, as he will win my love,
He bear himself with honourable action,
Such as he hath observ'd in noble ladies 110
Unto their lords, by them accomplishèd.
Such duty to the drunkard let him do
With soft low tongue and lowly courtesy,
And say 'What is't your Honour will command,
Wherein your lady and your humble wife 115
May show her duty and make known her love?'
And then with kind embracements, tempting kisses,
And with declining head into his bosom,
Bid him shed tears, as being overjoy'd
To see her noble lord restor'd to health, 120
Who, for this seven years hath, esteemed him
No better than a poor and loathsome beggar.
And if the boy have not a woman's gift
To rain a shower of commanded tears,
An onion will do well for such a shift, 125
Which, in a napkin being close convey'd,
Shall in despite enforce a watery eye.
See this dispatch'd with all the haste thou canst.
Anon I'll give thee more instructions.
[Exit a SERVINGMAN]
I know the boy will well usurp the grace, 130
Voice, gait, and action, of a gentlewoman.
I long to hear him call the drunkard "husband"!
And how my men will stay themselves from laughter
When they do homage to this simple peasant.
I'll in to counsel them. Haply my presence 135
May well abate the over-merry spleen
Which otherwise would grow into extremes.
[Exeunt]

LORD *[Lord to a SERVANT]* Escort them, sir, to the wine barrels in the storage room. Welcome each one. Offer them whatever they want. *[A SERVANT departs with the acting troupe.] [Lord to another servant]* Sir, find my errand boy Bartholomew and dress him in women's clothes. Take the boy to Christopher Sly's bedroom. Refer to Bartholomew as "madam" and bow to him. Tell Bartholomew to behave honorably if he wants to please me. Order him to imitate how ladies treat their husbands. Have Bartholomew speak softly and politely to the drunkard. And ask, "What do you want your wife to do to show her obedience and love?" Have Bartholomew caress and kiss Christopher Sly. Ask Bartholomew to bow his head and to weep in joy that the lord is cured. Note that the lord has believed himself to be a beggar for seven years. If the boy can't cry easily, put an onion in a cloth and hold it near his eyes to make them teary eyed. Hurry to your task. Soon I will give you more instructions. *[The SERVANT goes out.]* I know that Bartholomew will mimic the grace, voice, walk, and actions of a gentlewoman. I would love to hear Bartholomew call the drunkard "husband." I wonder how my staff will keep from laughing when they honor this simpleton Sly. I will go upstairs to give the staff advice. Perhaps my presence will keep them from bursting out laughing. *[The PLAYERS and the LORD go out.]*

INDUCTION, SCENE 2

A bedchamber in the LORD'S house.

[Enter aloft SLY with ATTENDANTS; some with apparel, basin, and ewer, and other appurtenances; and LORD, disguised as a servant]

SLY For God's sake, a pot of small ale.

FIRST SERVANT Will't please your Lordship drink a cup of sack?

SECOND SERVANT Will't please your Honour taste of these conserves?

THIRD SERVANT What raiment will your Honour wear today?

SLY I am Christophero Sly! Call not me 'Honour' nor 5
'Lordship.' I ne'er drank sack in my life. And if you
give me any conserves, give me conserves of beef.
Ne'er ask me what raiment I'll wear, for I have no
more doublets than backs, no more stockings than
legs, nor no more shoes than feet, nay, sometime more 10
feet than shoes, or such shoes as my toes look through
the over-leather.

LORD *[as SERVANT]* Heaven cease this idle humour in your
Honour!
O, that a mighty man of such descent,
Of such possessions, and so high esteem 15
Should be infusèd with so foul a spirit!

SLY What! would you make me mad? Am not I Christopher Sly, old
Sly's son of Burton-Heath, by birth a peddler,
by education a cardmaker, by transmutation a bearherd, and
now by present profession a tinker? Ask Marian 20
Hacket, the fat ale-wife of Wincot, if she know me not! If she
say I am not fourteen pence on the score for sheer ale, score
me up for the lyingest knave in Christendom.
[servant returns with a pot of ale] What! I am not bestraught.
Here's— *[SLY drinks]* 25

THIRD SERVANT O! This it is that makes your lady mourn.

SECOND SERVANT O! This is it that makes your servants droop.

INDUCTION, SCENE 2

A bedroom in the lord's house.

[SLY enters the second-floor stage gallery with servants. Some carry clothing. Others bring a basin, pitcher, and bathing essentials. The LORD arrives.]

SLY For God's sake, bring me a mug of ale.

FIRST SERVANT Would your lordship like a cup of sherry?

SECOND SERVANT Would your honor like a bit of fruit preserves?

THIRD SERVANT What garments will your honor wear today?

SLY I am Christopher Sly. Don't call me "your honor" or "lordship." I never drank sherry in my life. If you give me preserves, make it salt beef. Don't ask what clothing I will wear. I have no more vests than the one on my back, no more hose than one for each leg, and no more shoes than my two feet. Sometimes, I have more feet than shoes, or my toes stick out of the front.

LORD *[as a SERVANT]* Please halt this ridiculous fantasy, your honor! How can so important a man of such family, property, and prestige arouse so evil a temper!

SLY Are you trying to make me crazy? I am Christopher Sly, son of Sly of Burtonheath near Stratford. By birth, I'm a peddler. By training, I make carding combs for untangling wool. After a change of career, I became a bear tamer. Currently, I repair tin. Ask Marian Hacket, the fat barkeeper at Wincot, to identify me. If she doesn't identify me as a debtor owing fourteen pennies for beer, you can rate me the most dishonest rascal in all Christian countries. *[A servant returns with a pot of ale.]* Look, I am not crazed. Here is—*[SLY drinks]*

THIRD SERVANT These outbursts make your wife cry!

SECOND SERVANT This mania depresses your staff!

LORD Hence comes it that your kindred shuns your house,
As beaten hence by your strange lunacy.
O noble lord, bethink thee of thy birth, 30
Call home thy ancient thoughts from banishment,
And banish hence these abject lowly dreams.
Look how thy servants do attend on thee,
Each in his office ready at thy beck.
Wilt thou have music? Hark! Apollo plays, 35
[Music]
And twenty cagèd nightingales do sing.
Or wilt thou sleep? We'll have thee to a couch
Softer and sweeter than the lustful bed
On purpose trimm'd up for Semiramis.
Say thou wilt walk, we will bestrew the ground. 40
Or wilt thou ride? Thy horses shall be trapp'd,
Their harness studded all with gold and pearl.
Dost thou love hawking? Thou hast hawks will soar
Above the morning lark. Or wilt thou hunt?
Thy hounds shall make the welkin answer them 50
And fetch shrill echoes from the hollow earth.

FIRST SERVANT Say thou wilt course. Thy greyhounds are as swift
As breathèd stags, ay, fleeter than the roe.

SECOND SERVANT Dost thou love pictures? We will fetch thee straight
Adonis painted by a running brook, 55
And Cytherea all in sedges hid,
Which seem to move and wanton with her breath
Even as the waving sedges play with wind.

LORD We'll show thee Io as she was a maid
And how she was beguilèd and surpris'd, 60
As lively painted as the deed was done.

THIRD SERVANT Or Daphne roaming through a thorny wood,
Scratching her legs, that one shall swear she bleeds,
And at that sight shall sad Apollo weep,
So workmanly the blood and tears are drawn. 65

LORD Thou art a lord, and nothing but a lord;
Thou hast a lady far more beautiful
Than any woman in this waning age.

FIRST SERVANT And, till the tears that she hath shed for thee
Like envious floods o'errun her lovely face, 70
She was the fairest creature in the world,
And yet she is inferior to none.

LORD Because of your madness, your relatives stay away from your home. Noble lord, remember your worthy family tree. Return to your former sanity. Abandon these fantasies of peasant life. Look at all these servants around you, each awaiting your orders. Would you like music? Listen, the god Apollo plays for you. *[Music sounds.]* Twenty caged nightingales will sing for you. Would you rather sleep? We will carry you to a lounge softer and more fragrant than the bed made up for the lustful Queen Semiramis of Iraq. Do you want to take a walk? We will spread herbs on the path. Would you like a horseback ride? We will fit your horses with gold and pearl harness. Would you like to go hunting with your hawk? You have hunting birds that will soar over the skylark. Would you like to hunt to hounds? Your dog pack will bay into the sky a sound that will echo across the earth.

FIRST SERVANT Would you like to chase rabbits? Your greyhounds are as fast as stags, swifter than miniature deer.

SECOND SERVANT Would you like artworks? We will bring a portrait of the classic hunter Adonis painted by a stream. And pictures of Venus hidden on the banks in reeds that seem to quiver with her breathing while the wind blows.

LORD We will bring a picture of the classical beauty Io as a young girl. And show how Jupiter charmed and surprised her, as realistically painted as the courtship itself.

THIRD SERVANT Or a picture of Daphne wandering the tangled woods, where thorns scratched her legs bloody. At the sight of her pain, the sun god Apollo weeps tears that look real.

LORD You are truly an aristocrat. You have a wife more beautiful than any of our day.

FIRST SERVANT She weeps so much for you that tears flood her lovely cheeks. She was the prettiest woman in the world. Even in tears, no one is lovelier.

SLY Am I a lord? And have I such a lady?
Or do I dream? Or have I dream'd till now?
I do not sleep: I see, I hear, I speak, 75
I smell sweet savours, and I feel soft things.
Upon my life, I am a lord indeed
And not a tinker, nor Christopher Sly.
Well, bring our lady hither to our sight,
And once again, a pot o' the smallest ale. 80

SECOND SERVANT Will't please your mightiness to wash your hands?
[SERVANTS present a ewer, basin, and napkin]
O, how we joy to see your wit restor'd!
O, that once more you knew but what you are!
These fifteen years you have been in a dream,
Or, when you wak'd, so wak'd as if you slept. 85

SLY These fifteen years! By my fay, a goodly nap.
But did I never speak of all that time?

FIRST SERVANT O, yes, my lord, but very idle words.
For though you lay here in this goodly chamber,
Yet would you say you were beaten out of door, 90
And rail upon the hostess of the house,
And say you would present her at the leet
Because she brought stone jugs and no seal'd quarts.
Sometimes you would call out for Cicely Hacket.

SLY Ay, the woman's maid of the house. 95

THIRD SERVANT Why, sir, you know no house nor no such maid,
Nor no such men as you have reckon'd up,
As Stephen Sly, and old John Naps of Greet,
And Peter Turph, and Henry Pimpernell,
And twenty more such names and men as these, 100
Which never were, nor no man ever saw.

SLY Now, Lord be thanked for my good amends!

ALL Amen.

SLY I thank thee. Thou shalt not lose by it.
[Enter the PAGE, as a lady, with ATTENDANTS]

PAGE *[as a lady]* How fares my noble lord? 105

SLY Marry, I fare well, for here is cheer enough.
Where is my wife?

PAGE Here, noble lord. What is thy will with her?

SLY	Am I a lord? Am I married to a beautiful wife? Am I dreaming? Was I dreaming in my former life? I'm not asleep. I can see, hear, talk. I smell sweet fragrance and feel soft linens. I declare, I am a lord and not the tin repairman Christopher Sly. So, bring my wife here. I ask again for a mug of the weakest beer.
SECOND SERVANT	Would you like to wash your hands, mighty lord? *[SERVANTS present a pitcher, a basin, and a napkin.]* We are thrilled to see you sane again! You recognize your old self! For fifteen years, you have been deluded. Even when you were awake, you seemed dreamy.
SLY	For fifteen years? That was a long nap. Did I talk during that time?
FIRST SERVANT	Yes, you spoke, but only nonsense. Even though you lay in an elegant bedroom, you thought you were forced outdoors. You yelled at the barmaid. You threatened to sue her for serving homemade beer rather than quarts with official stamps. Sometimes you called for Cicely Hacket.
SLY	Yes, she is the alehouse chambermaid.
THIRD SERVANT	You don't know such a low alehouse or chambermaid. You don't know the names you mentioned—Stephen Sly, John Naps of Greece, Peter Turph, and Henry Pimpernell. You don't know any of the twenty people you mentioned. They don't even exist.
SLY	Thank God I am cured!
ALL	Amen to that.
SLY	I thank you all. I will reward you. *[The PAGE, dressed in women's clothes, enters with SERVANTS.]*
PAGE	How is my husband feeling?
SLY	I am doing well in this cheerful place. Where is my wife?
PAGE	Here I am, lord. What do you want?

SLY Are you my wife, and will not call me 'husband'?
My men should call me 'lord.' I am your goodman. 110

PAGE My husband and my lord, my lord and husband,
I am your wife in all obedience.

SLY I know it well. What must I call her?

LORD 'Madam.'

SLY 'Alice Madam,' or 'Joan Madam'? 115

LORD 'Madam,' and nothing else. So lords call ladies.

SLY Madam wife, they say that I have dream'd
And slept above some fifteen year or more.

PAGE Ay, and the time seems thirty unto me,
Being all this time abandon'd from your bed. 120

SLY 'Tis much. Servants, leave me and her alone.
Madam, undress you, and come now to bed.

PAGE Thrice noble lord, let me entreat of you
To pardon me yet for a night or two;
Or, if not so, until the sun be set. 125
For your physicians have expressly charg'd,
In peril to incur your former malady,
That I should yet absent me from your bed.
I hope this reason stands for my excuse.

SLY Ay, it stands so that I may hardly tarry so long; but I 130
would be loath to fall into my dreams again. I will therefore
tarry in despite of the flesh and the blood.
[Enter a SERVANT as a Messenger]

MESSENGER Your Honour's players, hearing your amendment,
Are come to play a pleasant comedy
For so your doctors hold it very meet, 135
Seeing too much sadness hath congeal'd your blood,
And melancholy is the nurse of frenzy.
Therefore they thought it good you hear a play
And frame your mind to mirth and merriment,
Which bars a thousand harms and lengthens life. 140

SLY Marry, I will. Let them play it. Is not a commonty a
Christmas gambold or a tumbling-trick?

PAGE No, my good lord; it is more pleasing stuff.

SLY Are you a wife who does not call me husband? My staff calls me "lord." You should call me "goodman."

PAGE You are my husband and lord, my lord and husband. I am your obedient wife.

SLY I know you are obedient. What should I call her?

LORD Call her "madam."

SLY Madam Alice or Madam Joan?

LORD Just call her "madam." That's how lords refer to their wives.

SLY Madam wife, the servants say that I have slept for over fifteen years.

PAGE It seems like thirty years since you banished me from your bed.

SLY It is a long time. Staff, leave me in private with her. Madam, undress and come to bed.

PAGE Lord, let me beg your leave to wait a night or two or at least until sundown. Your doctors have left orders to keep you from falling ill again. I must stay out of your bed. Please accept my reason.

SLY I can hardly wait that long. But I don't want to get sick again. I will wait in spite of my desire for you. *[A messenger arrives.]*

MESSENGER Your acting company has heard of your cure. They came to perform a comedy. Your doctors approve. They don't want a sad play to thicken your blood, or for depression to force you into mania. They suggest a play full of joy and fun. It will save you from harm and lengthen your life.

SLY I approve the entertainment. Isn't comedy a holiday frolic or an acrobatic trick?

PAGE No, sir. Comedy is more enjoyable.

SLY What! Household stuff?

PAGE It is a kind of history. 145

SLY Well, we'll see't. Come, madam wife, sit by my side and let the world slip.We shall ne'er be younger.
[They sit.]

SLY A domestic play?

PAGE Comedy is like history.

SLY We will watch it. Wife, sit by me and abandon your care. We will feel young again. *[Everyone sits. A trumpet fanfare introduces the play.]*

ACT I, SCENE 1

Padua. A public place.

[Flourish; Enter LUCENTIO and his man TRANIO]

LUCENTIO Tranio, since for the great desire I had
To see fair Padua, nursery of arts,
I am arriv'd for fruitful Lombardy,
The pleasant garden of great Italy,
And by my father's love and leave am arm'd 5
With his good will and thy good company.
My trusty servant well approv'd in all,
Here let us breathe and haply institute
A course of learning and ingenious studies.
Pisa, renowned for grave citizens, 10
Gave me my being and my father first,
A merchant of great traffic through the world,
Vincentio, come of the Bentivolii.
Vincentio's son, brought up in Florence,
It shall become to serve all hopes conceiv'd, 15
To deck his fortune with his virtuous deeds:
And therefore, Tranio, for the time I study
Virtue, and that part of philosophy
Will I apply that treats of happiness
By virtue specially to be achiev'd. 20
Tell me thy mind, for I have Pisa left
And am to Padua come, as he that leaves
A shallow plash to plunge him in the deep
And with satiety seeks to quench his thirst.

ACT I, SCENE 1

In a street before Baptista's house in Padua in northeastern Italy.

[A trumpet fanfare precedes the entrance of the wealthy youth LUCENTIO and his servant TRANIO.]

LUCENTIO Tranio, I have been longing to see Padua, a university city. I have come on my way to Lombardy, a fruitful section of north central Italy. My dear father willingly sent you to accompany me. My faithful servant, let us enroll in intellectual studies here. Pisa, which is known for serious citizens, is my hometown and that of my father Vincentio, a global merchant of the Bentivolii clan. It will please my father if I, brought up in Florence, elevate myself with great deeds. For now, Tranio, I study goodness and the area of philosophy concerning how to be happy through moral behavior. Tell me your thoughts on my departure from Pisa to Padua. I have left a shallow pond to dive into deep learning and to fulfill my longing for knowledge.

TRANIO Mi perdonato, gentle master mine. 25
I am in all affected as yourself,
Glad that you thus continue your resolve
To suck the sweets of sweet philosophy.
Only, good master, while we do admire
This virtue and this moral discipline, 30
Let's be no stoics nor no stocks, I pray,
Or so devote to Aristotle's checks
As Ovid be an outcast quite abjur'd.
Balk logic with acquaintance that you have,
And practise rhetoric in your common talk; 35
Music and poesy use to quicken you;
The mathematics and the metaphysics,
Fall to them as you find your stomach serves you.
No profit grows where is no pleasure ta'en.
In brief, sir, study what you most affect. 40

LUCENTIO Gramercies, Tranio, well dost thou advise.
If, Biondello, thou wert come ashore,
We could at once put us in readiness
And take a lodging fit to entertain
Such friends as time in Padua shall beget. 45
[Enter BAPTISTA with his two daughters, KATHERINA and BIANCA; GREMIO, a pantaloon, and HORTENSIO, suitors to Bianca]
But stay awhile! What company is this?

TRANIO Master, some show to welcome us to town.
[LUCENTIO and TRANIO stand by.]

BAPTISTA *[To Gremio and Hortensio]* Gentlemen, importune me no further,
For how I firmly am resolv'd you know:
That is, not to bestow my youngest daughter 50
Before I have a husband for the elder.
If either of you both love Katherina,
Because I know you well and love you well,
Leave shall you have to court her at your pleasure.

GREMIO To cart her rather. She's too rough for me. 55
There, there, Hortensio, will you any wife?

KATE *[To Baptista]* I pray you, sir, is it your will
To make a stale of me amongst these mates?

HORTENSIO 'Mates,' maid! How mean you that? No mates for you,
Unless you were of gentler, milder mould. 60

TRANIO Pardon me, my master. I share your longing for knowledge. I am glad that you intend to study philosophy. While we honor goodness and moral self-control, please, let's not be too stuffy or self-denying. Let's not devote ourselves so thoroughly to Aristotle's rules that we exile ourselves from society like Ovid, whom the Emperor Augustus banished. Practice arguments with your own logic and apply grammar to your everyday speech. Music and verse will stimulate you. Enjoy math and physics as much as you like. You will gain nothing from unpleasant study. Finally, Lucentio, study anything you want.

LUCENTIO Thanks, Tranio, for your good advice. When Biondello arrives, we will be all set. We can rent quarters suited to welcoming new friends from Padua. *[BAPTISTA and his daughters, KATHERINA and BIANCA, enter. Accompanying them are Bianca's suitors, the foolish GREMIO and HORTENSIO.]* Wait! Who is this approaching?

TRANIO Someone has come to welcome us to Padua, master. *[LUCENTIO and TRANIO observe the company.]*

BAPTISTA *[Baptista to Gremio and Hortensio]* Gentlemen, don't ask again. You know my decision. I won't betrothe my younger daughter before I find a husband for the older girl. If either of you love Katherina, I will allow you to court her because I know and approve of you.

GREMIO To parade her in a cart. She's too unruly for me. Hortensio, are you picky about choosing a wife?

KATE *[Kate to her father Baptista]* Are you trying to ridicule me in front of these rowdies?

HORTENSIO "Rowdies," ma'am! What do you mean by that? You will have no suitors unless you become gentle and even-tempered.

KATE I' faith, sir, you shall never need to fear.
Iwis it is not halfway to her heart.
But if it were, doubt not her care should be
To comb your noddle with a three-legg'd stool
And paint your face and use you like a fool. 65

HORTENSIO From all such devils, good Lord deliver us!

GREMIO And me, too, good Lord!

TRANIO *[To LUCENTIO]* Hush, master! Here's some good pastime toward;
That wench is stark mad or wonderful froward.

LUCENTIO But in the other's silence do I see 70
Maid's mild behaviour and sobriety.
Peace, Tranio!

TRANIO Well said, master. Mum, and gaze your fill.

BAPTISTA *[To HORTENSIO and GREMIO]* Gentlemen, that I may soon make good
What I have said—Bianca, get you in, 75
And let it not displease thee, good Bianca,
For I will love thee ne'er the less, my girl.

KATE A pretty peat! It is best
Put finger in the eye, an she knew why.

BIANCA Sister, content you in my discontent. 80
Sir, to your pleasure humbly I subscribe.
My books and instruments shall be my company,
On them to look, and practice by myself.

LUCENTIO Hark, Tranio! Thou mayst hear Minerva speak.

HORTENSIO Signior Baptista, will you be so strange? 85
Sorry am I that our good will effects
Bianca's grief.

GREMIO Why will you mew her up,
Signior Baptista, for this fiend of hell,
And make her bear the penance of her tongue? 90

KATE You needn't worry about that. I am not even half interested in courtship. If I were interested in you, I would want to rake you over the head with a three-legged stool and rip your face with scratches and treat you like a clown.

HORTENSIO From so devilish a woman, Lord spare us!

GREMIO Me, too, Lord!

TRANIO *[TRANIO to his master LUCENTIO]* Don't say anything, Lucentio! This conversation will be fun to watch. That woman is either raving or awfully outspoken.

LUCENTIO In the sister Bianca's silence I observe a mild, serious girl. Quiet, Tranio!

TRANIO Good choice, Lucentio. Stay quiet and look at her all you want.

BAPTISTA *[BAPTISTA to HORTENSIO and GREMIO]* Gentlemen, to achieve what I have in mind—Bianca, go indoors. Don't feel slighted, Bianca. I love you as much as I love Kate.

KATE A spoiled pet! If she understood your meaning, she might as well poke herself in the eye.

BIANCA Kate, enjoy my displeasure. Father, I do what you ask. In solitude, I will read and play musical instruments.

LUCENTIO Notice, Tranio, that Bianca speaks like wise Minerva.

HORTENSIO Baptista, why are you so harsh to Bianca? I regret that our courtship causes Bianca unhappiness.

GREMIO Why do you confine Bianca, Baptista, and seek a husband for the fiendish Kate? Why should Bianca suffer for Kate's evil words?

BAPTISTA Gentlemen, content you. I am resolv'd.
Go in, Bianca.
[Exit BIANCA]
And for I know she taketh most delight
In music, instruments, and poetry,
Schoolmasters will I keep within my house 95
Fit to instruct her youth. If you, Hortensio,
Or, Signior Gremio, you, know any such,
Prefer them hither. For to cunning men
I will be very kind, and liberal
To mine own children in good bringing up. 100
And so, farewell. Katherina, you may stay,
For I have more to commune with Bianca.
[Exit]

KATE Why, and I trust I may go too, may I not?
What! Shall I be appointed hours, as though, belike,
I knew not what to take and what to leave? Ha! 105
[Exit]

GREMIO You may go to the devil's dam! Your gifts are so good here's none will hold you. Their love is not so great, Hortensio, but we may blow our nails together, and fast it fairly out. Our cake's dough on both sides. Farewell. Yet, for the love I bear my sweet Bianca, if I can by any means 110 light on a fit man to teach her that wherein she delights, I will wish him to her father.

HORTENSIO So will I, Signior Gremio. But a word, I pray. Though the nature of our quarrel yet never brooked parle, know now upon advice, it toucheth us both—that we may yet again 115 have access to our fair mistress, and be happy rivals in Bianca's love—to labour and effect one thing specially.

GREMIO What's that, I pray?

HORTENSIO Marry, sir, to get a husband for her sister.

GREMIO A husband? A devil! 120

HORTENSIO I say, 'a husband.'

GREMIO I say, 'a devil.' Thinkest thou, Hortensio, though her Father be very rich, any man is so very a fool to be married to hell?

BAPTISTA Gentleman, enough. I won't change my mind. Bianca, go indoors. *[BIANCA exits.]*
I know how much Bianca likes music and verse. I will hire tutors to instruct her at home. If you, Hortensio and Gremio, know any tutors for hire, recommend them to me. To clever men I am hospitable. I am generous to my growing children. Goodbye to you both. Katherina, you may stay here. I want to talk privately with Bianca.
[BAPTISTA goes out.]

KATE And I can go where I want, can't I? Well, will you give me curfews as though I didn't know how to behave? Ha!
[KATE goes out.]

GREMIO You may go to Satan's mother! You are so free that no one can restrain you. Our desire for them is not so strong, Hortensio. We can twiddle our thumbs and do without women. We failed to persuade Baptista. Goodbye. Because I love Bianca, if I can find a tutor in her favorite subjects, I will recommend him to Baptista.

HORTENSIO So will I, Gremio. I ask a private word. Although our rivalry never resulted in an argument, just remember, this matter of a husband for Katherina concerns both of us. We may once more court our fair lady and compete for Bianca's hand. We must once more work toward one aim.

GREMIO What aim is that?

HORTENSIO Sir, to find a husband for Kate.

GREMIO A husband? She deserves a demon!

HORTENSIO I insist we find her a husband.

GREMIO I repeat, she deserves a demon. Do you think, Hortensio, just because Baptista is wealthy that any man is fool enough to marry a devilish heiress?

HORTENSIO Tush, Gremio! Though it pass your patience and mine to endure her loud alarums, why, man, there be good fellows in the world, an a man could light on them, would take her with all faults, and money enough. 125

GREMIO I cannot tell. But I had as lief take her dowry with this condition: to be whipp'd at the high cross every morning. 130

HORTENSIO Faith, as you say, there's small choice in rotten apples.
But, come, since this bar in law makes us friends, it shall be so far forth friendly maintained till by helping
Baptista's eldest daughter to a husband, we set his youngest free for a husband, and then have to't afresh. 135
Sweet Bianca! Happy man be his dole! He that runs fastest gets the ring. How say you, Signior Gremio?

GREMIO I am agreed; and would I had given him the best horse in Padua to begin his wooing, that would thoroughly woo her, wed her, and bed her, and rid the house of her. 140
Come on.
[Exeunt GREMIO and HORTENSIO]

TRANIO I pray, sir, tell me, is it possible
That love should of a sudden take such hold?

LUCENTIO O Tranio! Till I found it to be true,
I never thought it possible or likely. 145
But see, while idly I stood looking on,
I found the effect of love in idleness,
And now in plainness do confess to thee
That art to me as secret and as dear
As Anna to the Queen of Carthage was: 150
Tranio, I burn, I pine! I perish, Tranio,
If I achieve not this young modest girl.
Counsel me, Tranio, for I know thou canst:
Assist me, Tranio, for I know thou wilt.

TRANIO Master, it is no time to chide you now. 155
Affection is not rated from the heart.
If love have touch'd you, naught remains but so:
'Redime te captum, quam queas minimo.'

LUCENTIO Gramercies, lad. Go forward. This contents;
The rest will comfort, for thy counsel's sound. 160

TRANIO Master, you look'd so longly on the maid,
Perhaps you mark'd not what's the pith of all.

HORTENSIO Hush, Gremio! You and I are too unwilling to tolerate Kate's loud mouth. There are men in the world we could find who would endure Kate's faults for the sake of Baptista's money.

GREMIO I don't know any such man. I would take Kate's dowry on one condition: To be lashed at the cross in the center of town every morning.

HORTENSIO Indeed, we have little to choose from among rotten apples. Since Baptista's edict makes us rivals for Bianca, let us work together. We will locate a husband for Kate until we set Bianca free to marry. Then we can begin courting Bianca once more. Sweet girl! Any man would be happy to have her! The man who is quickest wins the prize. Do you agree, Gremio?

GREMIO I agree. I would bribe Kate's suitor with the best horse in Padua. For the horse, he would have to court, marry, and bed her and rid Baptista's house of her. Let's go. *[GREMIO and HORTENSIO depart.]*

TRANIO Please, Lucentio, could you fall in love that quickly?

LUCENTIO Tranio, until it happened to me, I never believed it possible or likely. While I watched from here, I felt the magic of instant infatuation. I tell you straight, because you are as trusted a friend as Anna was to her sister Dido, Queen of Carthage. Tranio, I ache, I yearn for Bianca! I will die, Tranio, if I don't marry this young maid. Advise me, Tranio. I know you are wise. Help me, Tranio. I know you are willing.

TRANIO Master, I shouldn't scold you now. I can't force love from your heart. If you are really in love, there is only one solution: "Buy yourself back as cheaply as you can."

LUCENTIO Thanks, Tranio. Walk on. I am pleased with your reply. I take comfort in your sound wisdom.

TRANIO Lucentio, you looked so long at Bianca that maybe you missed the rest of the conversation.

LUCENTIO O, yes, I saw sweet beauty in her face,
Such as the daughter of Agenor had,
That made great Jove to humble him to her hand 165
When with his knees he kiss'd the Cretan strand.

TRANIO Saw you no more? Mark'd you not how her sister
Began to scold and raise up such a storm
That mortal ears might hardly endure the din?

LUCENTIO Tranio, I saw her coral lips to move, 170
And with her breath she did perfume the air.
Sacred and sweet was all I saw in her.

TRANIO Nay, then, 'tis time to stir him from his trance.
I pray, awake, sir! If you love the maid,
Bend thoughts and wits to achieve her. Thus it stands: 175
Her elder sister is so curst and shrewd
That till the father rid his hands of her,
Master, your love must live a maid at home,
And therefore has he closely mew'd her up,
Because she will not be annoy'd with suitors. 180

LUCENTIO Ah, Tranio, what a cruel father's he!
But art thou not advis'd he took some care
To get her cunning schoolmasters to instruct her?

TRANIO Ay, marry, am I, sir, and now 'tis plotted.

LUCENTIO I have it, Tranio!

TRANIO Master, for my hand, 185
Both our inventions meet and jump in one.

LUCENTIO Tell me thine first.

TRANIO You will be schoolmaster
And undertake the teaching of the maid:
That's your device.

LUCENTIO It is. May it be done?

TRANIO Not possible. For who shall bear your part 190
And be in Padua here Vincentio's son,
Keep house and ply his book, welcome his friends,
Visit his countrymen, and banquet them?

LUCENTIO I saw Bianca's sweet loveliness. She is as beautiful as Agenor's daughter Europa, who brought Jupiter to his knees as soon as he arrived in Crete.

TRANIO Is that all you saw? Didn't you notice how her sister Kate fumed and fussed enough to deafen you?

LUCENTIO I saw Bianca's pink lips open and her breath sweeten the air. I saw a pure, sweet girl.

TRANIO I must jolt you from your dream world. Wake up, Lucentio. If you love Bianca, you have to think up a way to win her. This is what you must do: Her older sister Kate is so foul-tempered and cunning, till Baptista gets rid of her, you must remain a bachelor. Baptista has confined Bianca at home away from all suitors.

LUCENTIO Tranio, Baptista is a cruel father! But didn't he promise to hire clever tutors for Bianca?

TRANIO Aha, Lucentio, I see a way to get Bianca.

LUCENTIO I know what to do, Tranio!

TRANIO I guarantee, master, that we are both thinking the same thing.

LUCENTIO Tell me your scheme.

TRANIO You will pose as a tutor and begin teaching Bianca. That's your plan.

LUCENTIO That's it. Will it succeed?

TRANIO It won't work. Who will pose as Lucentio, Vincentio's son, in Padua? Who will rent a house, study, entertain friends, visit fellow Pisans, and invite them to dinner?

LUCENTIO Basta, content thee, for I have it full.
We have not yet been seen in any house, 195
Nor can we be distinguish'd by our faces
For man or master. Then it follows thus:
Thou shalt be master, Tranio, in my stead,
Keep house and port and servants, as I should.
I will some other be, some Florentine, 200
Some Neapolitan, or meaner man of Pisa.
'Tis hatch'd, and shall be so. Tranio, at once
Uncase thee. Take my colour'd hat and cloak.
[They exchange habits.]
When Biondello comes, he waits on thee,
But I will charm him first to keep his tongue. 205

TRANIO So had you need.
In brief, sir, sith it your pleasure is,
And I am tied to be obedient
For so your father charg'd me at our parting:
'Be serviceable to my son,' quoth he, 210
Although I think 'twas in another sense,
I am content to be Lucentio,
Because so well I love Lucentio.

LUCENTIO Tranio, be so, because Lucentio loves,
And let me be a slave, to achieve that maid 215
Whose sudden sight hath thrall'd my wounded eye.
[Enter BIONDELLO]
Here comes the rogue.—Sirrah, where have you been?

BIONDELLO Where have I been? Nay, how now! Where are you?
Master, has my fellow Tranio stol'n your clothes?
Or you stol'n his? Or both? Pray, what's the news? 220

LUCENTIO Sirrah, come hither. 'Tis no time to jest,
And therefore frame your manners to the time.
Your fellow Tranio here, to save my life,
Puts my apparel and my count'nance on,
And I for my escape have put on his; 225
For in a quarrel since I came ashore
I kill'd a man and fear I was descried.
Wait you on him, I charge you, as becomes,
While I make way from hence to save my life.
You understand me?

BIONDELLO I, sir? Ne'er a whit. 230

LUCENTIO And not a jot of Tranio in your mouth.
Tranio is changed to Lucentio.

LUCENTIO Enough quibbling. I see the whole plan. No one in Padua has received us. No one knows servant from master. This is what we will do. You will play the part of master, Tranio. Rent a house, entertain, and hire servants as I would. I will pose as a citizen of Florence or Naples or as a low-class Pisan. That's it. That's what we'll do. Tranio, undress and wear my hat and cape. *[LUCENTIO and TRANIO exchange outfits.]* When Biondello arrives, he will be your servant. I will warn him first to guard our secret.

TRANIO You should alert him. In short, Lucentio, I must obey your wishes. Vincentio told me when we left Pisa, "Serve my son." But I don't think that's what he meant. I will enjoy being Lucentio, the master I admire.

LUCENTIO Play my role, Tranio, for I admire you. Even if I have to be a slave to win Bianca, who won me at first sight. *[BIONDELLO enters.]* Here comes that rascal. Biondello, where have you been?

BIONDELLO Where have I been? What is this? Why are you changed, Lucentio? Has Tranio stolen your clothes? Have you stolen his? Did both of you steal outfits? What is happening here?

LUCENTIO Come with us, Biondello. This is no time for joking. Behave like a servant. Tranio is saving my life by dressing like me and taking my identity. To escape danger, I wear Tranio's clothes. When I arrived in Padua, I killed a man. I am afraid someone saw me. Be his servant as though he were me. I must escape to save myself. Do you understand?

BIONDELLO Me? Not a bit.

LUCENTIO Don't call him Tranio. He is now Lucentio.

BIONDELLO The better for him. Would I were so too!

TRANIO So could I, faith, boy, to have the next wish after,
That Lucentio indeed had Baptista's youngest daughter. 235
But, sirrah, not for my sake but your master's, I advise
You use your manners discreetly in all kind of companies.
When I am alone, why, then I am Tranio;
But in all places else, your master, Lucentio.

LUCENTIO Tranio, let's go. 240
One thing more rests, that thyself execute,
To make one among these wooers. If thou ask me why,
Sufficeth my reasons are both good and weighty.
[Exeunt]
[The Induction Presenters speak.]

FIRST SERVANT My lord, you nod. You do not mind the play.

SLY Yes, by Saint Anne, do I. A good matter, surely. Comes 245
there any more of it?

PAGE My lord, 'tis but begun.

SLY 'Tis a very excellent piece of work, madam lady. Would 'twere
done!
[They sit and mark.]

BIONDELLO He's come up in status. I wish I were Lucentio.

TRANIO And I wish that Lucentio had Baptista's younger daughter Bianca. Biondello, for Lucentio's safety, be careful what you say wherever you are. In private, you may call me Tranio. In public, I am your master Lucentio.

LUCENTIO Tranio, let's go. I want you to join the other two suitors. I have good reason to ask you. *[LUCENTIO, TRANIO, and BIONDELLO depart.] [Characters in the introduction interrupt the comedy.]*

FIRST SERVANT My lord, you are dozing. You are not watching the play.

SLY Yes, by Saint Anne, Jesus's grandmother, I am watching. A good performance. Is there more?

PAGE My lord, this was only Act I.

SLY It is an excellent comedy, my lady. I wish it were finished! *[CHRISTOPHER SLY and BARTHOLOMEW turn their attention back to the play.]*

ACT I, SCENE 2

Padua. Before HORTENSIO'S house.

[Enter PETRUCHIO and his man GRUMIO]

PETRUCHIO Verona, for a while I take my leave,
To see my friends in Padua, but of all
My best beloved and approvèd friend,
Hortensio. And I trow this is his house.
Here, sirrah Grumio, knock, I say. 5

GRUMIO Knock, sir? Whom should I knock? Is there any man has rebused your Worship?

PETRUCHIO Villain, I say, knock me here soundly.

GRUMIO Knock you here, sir? Why, sir, what am I, sir, that I should knock you here, sir? 10

PETRUCHIO Villain, I say, knock me at this gate
And rap me well, or I'll knock your knave's pate.

GRUMIO My master is grown quarrelsome. I should knock you first, And then I know after who comes by the worst.

PETRUCHIO Will it not be? 15
Faith, sirrah, an you'll not knock, I'll ring it.
I'll try how you can sol, fa, and sing it.
[He wrings GRUMIO by the ears.]

GRUMIO Help, masters, help! My master is mad.

PETRUCHIO Now, knock when I bid you, sirrah villain!
[Enter HORTENSIO]

HORTENSIO How now! What's the matter? My old friend Grumio and my good friend Petruchio! How do you all at Verona? 20

PETRUCHIO Signior Hortensio, come you to part the fray?
Con tutto il cuore ben trovato, may I say.

HORTENSIO Alla nostra casa ben venuto,
Molto honorato signor mio Petruchio. 25
Rise, Grumio, rise. We will compound this quarrel.

ACT I, SCENE 2

In Padua in front of Hortensio's house.

[PETRUCHIO and his servant GRUMIO enter.]

PETRUCHIO I left Verona and traveled east to visit friends in Padua. My best friend in town is Hortensio. I believe that this is his house. Grumio, knock.

GRUMIO Knock, sir? Whom should I thump? Has someone insulted your worship?

PETRUCHIO Idiot, knock here.

GRUMIO Thump you here, sir? Why would I dare thump you?

PETRUCHIO Knock on this gate, fool. And knock hard or I will thump your stupid head.

GRUMIO Petruchio is grouchy. I should thump you first. Then I will suffer for it.

PETRUCHIO Aren't you listening? If you don't knock at the gate, I'll ring the bell. I'll squeeze notes out of you. *[He grasps GRUMIO's ears.]*

GRUMIO Help, my master has gone crazy.

PETRUCHIO Knock when I tell you, you lout! *[HORTENSIO enters.]*

HORTENSIO What's this noise? What's happening? It's Grumio and my old friend Petruchio! How is Verona?

PETRUCHIO Hortensio, did you come to halt the tussle? With all my heart, I find you well.

HORTENSIO Welcome to my house, my most honored friend Petruchio. Get up, Grumio. We will settle this argument.

GRUMIO	Nay, 'tis no matter, sir, what he 'leges in Latin. If this be not a lawful cause for me to leave his service, look you, sir; he bid me knock him and rap him soundly, sir. Well, was it fit for a servant to use his master so, being perhaps, for aught I see, two-and-thirty, a pip out? Whom, would to God, I had well knock'd at first, Then had not Grumio come by the worst.	 30
PETRUCHIO	A senseless villain! Good Hortensio, I bade the rascal knock upon your gate And could not get him for my heart to do it.	 35
GRUMIO	Knock at the gate? O heavens! Spake you not these words plain: 'Sirrah knock me here, rap me here, knock me well, and knock me soundly'? And come you now with 'knocking at the gate'?	 40
PETRUCHIO	Sirrah, be gone, or talk not, I advise you.	
HORTENSIO	Petruchio, patience. I am Grumio's pledge. Why, this's a heavy chance 'twixt him and you, Your ancient, trusty, pleasant servant Grumio. And tell me now, sweet friend, what happy gale Blows you to Padua here from old Verona?	 45
PETRUCHIO	Such wind as scatters young men through the world To seek their fortunes farther than at home, Where small experience grows. But in a few, Signior Hortensio, thus it stands with me: Antonio, my father, is deceas'd, And I have thrust myself into this maze, Happily to wive and thrive as best I may. Crowns in my purse I have, and goods at home, And so am come abroad to see the world.	 50 55
HORTENSIO	Petruchio, shall I then come roundly to thee And wish thee to a shrewd ill-favour'd wife? Thou'dst thank me but a little for my counsel; And yet I'll promise thee she shall be rich, And very rich. But th'art too much my friend, And I'll not wish thee to her.	 60

GRUMIO It isn't important, sir, whatever he told you in Latin. I have legal justification for leaving his service. He asked me thump him and hit him soundly, sir. Is it reasonable for a servant to mistreat his master, even if he is short a spot on a playing card? I wish that I had knocked on the gate when he told me. Then I would not have suffered his anger.

PETRUCHIO Witless knothead! Hortensio, I ordered Grumio to knock at your gate. I couldn't convince him to obey me.

GRUMIO Knock at the gate? Oh, God, is this not what you said! "You, knock here, thump me here, knock well, and rap soundly." You have changed the original words to "knocking at the gate."

PETRUCHIO I advise you to go away and say nothing.

HORTENSIO Petruchio, be patient with him. I speak for Grumio. Those were harsh words between you and your long-term servant, good-natured Grumio. What wind blows you from Verona east to Padua?

PETRUCHIO I follow the path of a young man seeking my fortune and gaining experience away from home. In a few words, Hortensio, this is the situation: My father Antonio died. I have forced myself into life to marry and prosper as well as I can. I have gold coins in my purse and an inheritance at home. I left to see the world.

HORTENSIO May I speak directly, Petruchio? Would you like a crafty, ill-tempered wife? You will resist my advice. But I promise she will be very wealthy. But you are too good a friend. I wouldn't wish her on you.

PETRUCHIO Signior Hortensio, 'twixt such friends as we
Few words suffice. And therefore, if thou know
One rich enough to be Petruchio's wife—
As wealth is burden of my wooing dance— 65
Be she as foul as was Florentius' love,
As old as Sibyl, and as curst and shrewd
As Socrates' Xanthippe or a worse,
She moves me not, or not removes, at least,
Affection's edge in me, were she as rough 70
As are the swelling Adriatic seas.
I come to wive it wealthily in Padua;
If wealthily, then happily in Padua.

GRUMIO Nay, look you, sir, he tells you flatly what his mind is. Why,
give him gold enough and marry him to a puppet or 75
an aglet-baby, or an old trot with ne'er a tooth in her head,
though she have as many diseases as two-and-fifty horses.
Why, nothing comes amiss, so money comes withal.

HORTENSIO Petruchio, since we are stepp'd thus far in, 80
I will continue that I broach'd in jest.
I can, Petruchio, help thee to a wife
With wealth enough, and young and beauteous,
Brought up as best becomes a gentlewoman.
Her only fault, and that is faults enough, 85
Is that she is intolerable curst
And shrewd and froward, so beyond all measure
That, were my state far worser than it is,
I would not wed her for a mine of gold.

PETRUCHIO Hortensio, peace! Thou know'st not gold's effect. 90
Tell me her father's name, and 'tis enough;
For I will board her, though she chide as loud
As thunder when the clouds in autumn crack.

HORTENSIO Her father is Baptista Minola,
An affable and courteous gentleman. Her name is
Katherina Minola, 95
Renown'd in Padua for her scolding tongue.

PETRUCHIO I know her father, though I know not her;
And he knew my deceased father well.
I will not sleep, Hortensio, till I see her;
And therefore let me be thus bold with you 100
To give you over at this first encounter,
Unless you will accompany me thither.

PETRUCHIO Hortensio, we are such old friends that we can be brief. If you know a woman rich enough to entice Petruchio—since financial gain is the object of my courtship—even if she is as grotesque as the Knight Florentius's hag, as ancient as the Roman prophetess, and as sour and suspicious as the philosopher Socrates's wife Xanthippe or worse, she will give me no trouble or dull my desire. Even if she were as harsh as waves on the Adriatic Sea. I came to Padua to find a rich wife. If she is rich, then I will happily marry in Padua.

GRUMIO Petruchio tells you his intent straight out. For enough money, he would marry a doll, or a shoelace ornament, or a toothless prostitute, even though she were as diseased as fifty-two horses. Nothing bothers Petruchio so long as he profits.

HORTENSIO Since we've gone this far, Petruchio, I will speak seriously. I will help you court a woman who is rich as well as young and pretty. She was reared a gentlewoman. Her only fault is her unbearable, cunning, and loud mouth. She is so unbearable that, even if I were poorer, I would not marry her for a gold mine.

PETRUCHIO Hortensio, say no more! You don't know how much I want wealth. Tell me her father's name. That's all I need to know. I will have her if she scolds like thunder through autumn clouds.

HORTENSIO Her father is Baptista Minola, a friendly and polite gentleman. She is Katherina Minola, known in Padua for her harsh words.

PETRUCHIO I know Baptista, but I don't know Katherina. Baptista knew my father well. I won't rest until I see her, Hortensio. I will abandon your friendship unless you take me to her.

GRUMIO *[To HORTENSIO]* I pray you, sir, let him go while the humour lasts. O' my word, an she knew him as well as I do, she would think scolding would do little good upon 105
him. She may perhaps call him half a score knaves or so. Why, that's nothing; and he begin once, he'll rail in his rope-tricks. I'll tell you what, sir, an she stand him
but a little, he will throw a figure in her face and so disfigure her with it that she shall have no more eyes to 110
see withal than a cat. You know him not, sir.

HORTENSIO Tarry, Petruchio, I must go with thee,
For in Baptista's keep my treasure is.
He hath the jewel of my life in hold,
His youngest daughter, beautiful Bianca, 115
And her withholds from me and other more,
Suitors to her and rivals in my love,
Supposing it a thing impossible,
For those defects I have before rehears'd,
That ever Katherina will be woo'd. 120
Therefore this order hath Baptista ta'en,
That none shall have access unto Bianca
Till Katherine the curst have got a husband.

GRUMIO Katherine the curst!
A title for a maid, of all titles the worst. 125

HORTENSIO Now shall my friend Petruchio do me grace
And offer me disguis'd in sober robes
To old Baptista as a schoolmaster
Well seen in music, to instruct Bianca,
That so I may, by this device at least, 130
Have leave and leisure to make love to her
And unsuspected court her by herself.

GRUMIO Here's no knavery! See, to beguile the old folks,
how the young folks lay their heads together!
[Enter GREMIO, and LUCENTIO disguised as Cambio the schoolmaster, with books under his arm]
Master, master, look about you. Who goes there, ha? 135

HORTENSIO Peace, Grumio, 'tis the rival of my love. Petruchio,
stand by awhile.
[PETRUCHIO, HORTENSIO, and GRUMIO stand aside.]

GRUMIO A proper stripling, and an amorous!

GRUMIO *[GRUMIO to HORTENSIO]* Please, sir, let him go to her while he is in good humor. If she knew him as well as I do, she would realize that nagging has no effect on him. she may call him ten times a criminal. It won't matter to him. He will begin reeling her in. If she tolerates him at all, he will so charm and overpower her that she will be blinded by him. You don't know this side of him, sir.

HORTENSIO Wait, Petruchio. I must go along, because in Baptista's house is my beloved. He holds my treasure, his younger daughter, the lovely Bianca. He keeps her from me and from other suitors, all my rivals. They think it impossible to marry off Katherina because of all the faults I told you about. Baptista has vowed that no one may court Bianca until Katherina marries.

GRUMIO Katherina the cursed! The worst of titles for a girl.

HORTENSIO Petruchio do me a favor. Present me in disguise to Baptista as a music tutor come to teach Bianca. In this mode, I can be near enough to woo her without interruption by rivals.

GRUMIO This is no crime! Young people plot to fool the older generation! *[GREMIO enters with LUCENTIO, who carries books and wears the disguise of Cambio the tutor.]* Hortensio, look quick. Who is that?

HORTENSIO Quiet, Grumio. It is my rival Lucentio. Petruchio, let's eavesdrop. *[PETRUCHIO, HORTENSIO, and GRUMIO stand nearby.]*

GRUMIO Lucentio is a handsome youth eager to court!

GREMIO *[To LUCENTIO]* O, very well; I have perus'd the note.
Hark you, sir, I'll have them very fairly bound, 140
All books of love. See that at any hand,
And see you read no other lectures to her.
You understand me. Over and beside
Signior Baptista's liberality,
I'll mend it with a largess. Take your papers too. 145
And let me have them very well perfum'd,
For she is sweeter than perfume itself
To whom they go to. What will you read to her?

LUCENTIO Whate'er I read to her, I'll plead for you
As for my patron, stand you so assur'd, 150
As firmly as yourself were still in place,
Yea, and perhaps with more successful words
Than you, unless you were a scholar, sir.

GREMIO O this learning, what a thing it is!

GRUMIO O this woodcock, what an ass it is! 155

PETRUCHIO Peace, sirrah!

HORTENSIO Grumio, mum! God save you, Signior Gremio!

GREMIO And you are well met, Signior Hortensio.
Trow you whither I am going? To Baptista Minola.
I promis'd to enquire carefully 160
About a schoolmaster for the fair Bianca,
And by good fortune I have lighted well
On this young man, for learning and behaviour
Fit for her turn, well read in poetry
And other books, good ones, I warrant you. 165

HORTENSIO 'Tis well. And I have met a gentleman
Hath promis'd me to help me to another,
A fine musician to instruct our mistress.
So shall I no whit be behind in duty
To fair Bianca, so belov'd of me. 170

GREMIO Belov'd of me, and that my deeds shall prove.

GRUMIO *[aside]* And that his bags shall prove.

GREMIO *[GREMIO to LUCENTIO]* Okay. I have examined the note. Notice, Lucentio, I want these books on love well bound. At any cost, read to her only of romance. Listen to me. In addition to Baptista's generosity, I will supplement her dowry with a gift. Take your instructions along. Let me perfume them, for she is sweeter than cologne. What will you read to her?

LUCENTIO Whatever I choose to read, be sure that I'll follow your advice as carefully as though you were still my servant. Perhaps I will use more winning words than you, even if you were a scholar.

GREMIO Oh, an intellectual, what a wonderful thing!

GRUMIO Oh, a snipe, what a jerk he is!

PETRUCHIO Hush, Grumio!

HORTENSIO Greetings, Gremio!

GREMIO It is good to see you, Hortensio. Do you know where I'm going? To Baptista Minola. I promised to look for a tutor for Bianca. With luck, I found this young man. I guarantee that, for education and courtesy, he suits Bianca. He is well read in verse and other good books.

HORTENSIO Excellent. I have met a man who will lead me to another tutor, a musician to train Bianca. I will remain true to Bianca, whom I love.

GREMIO I love her, too, as my actions will prove.

GRUMIO *[GRUMIO to himself]* And that his wallet will prove.

HORTENSIO Gremio, 'tis now no time to vent our love.
Listen to me, and if you speak me fair
I'll tell you news indifferent good for either. 175
[Introducing PETRUCHIO]
Here is a gentleman whom by chance I met,
Upon agreement from us to his liking,
Will undertake to woo curst Katherine,
Yea, and to marry her, if her dowry please.

GREMIO So said, so done, is well. 180
Hortensio, have you told him all her faults?

PETRUCHIO I know she is an irksome brawling scold.
If that be all, masters, I hear no harm.

GREMIO No? Say'st me so, friend? What countryman?

PETRUCHIO Born in Verona, old Antonio's son. 185
My father dead, my fortune lives for me,
And I do hope good days and long to see.

GREMIO O Sir, such a life with such a wife were strange!
But if you have a stomach, to't i' God's name;
You shall have me assisting you in all. 190
But will you woo this wildcat?

PETRUCHIO Will I live?

GRUMIO Will he woo her? Ay, or I'll hang her.

PETRUCHIO Why came I hither but to that intent?
Think you a little din can daunt mine ears? 195
Have I not in my time heard lions roar?
Have I not heard the sea, puff'd up with winds,
Rage like an angry boar chafèd with sweat?
Have I not heard great ordnance in the field
And heaven's artillery thunder in the skies? 200
Have I not in a pitched battle heard
Loud 'larums, neighing steeds, and trumpets clang?
And do you tell me of a woman's tongue,
That gives not half so great a blow to hear
As will a chestnut in a farmer's fire? 205
Tush, tush! Fear boys with bugs.

GRUMIO *[aside]* For he fears none.

GREMIO Hortensio, hark.
This gentleman is happily arriv'd,
My mind presumes, for his own good and ours. 210

HORTENSIO Gremio, this is no time to proclaim our love for Bianca. Listen to me. If you tell the truth, I will disclose news equally good for either of use. *[HORTENSIO introduces PETRUCHIO to GREMIO.]*
Here is a gentlemen I just met. If he likes our terms, he will court the foul-tempered Katherina. He will even wed her, if her dowry suits him.

GREMIO If that is true, well done. Hortensio, have you divulged all her faults?

PETRUCHIO I know that she is an annoying, raging nag. If those are her only faults, I'm not worried.

GREMIO No? Are you telling the truth, friend? Where are you from?

PETRUCHIO I am the son of Antonio of Verona. He died, leaving me his wealth. I hope to live a long, prosperous life.

GREMIO Oh, Petruchio, a long and prosperous life with a woman like Katherina would be rare! But if you have a taste for such a wife, go to it. I will be glad to help you. Will you romance this wildcat?

PETRUCHIO Will I survive?

GRUMIO Will he romance her? Yes, or I'll execute her.

PETRUCHIO Why did I come here except to romance her? Do you think a little snarling will bother me? I have heard lions before. Haven't I heard the angry sea like a sweating, raw-chapped boar? Haven't I heard cannon in combat and thunder in the sky? In war, haven't I heard trumpet calls, snorting horses, and trumpet blares? Do you describe a nagging woman who makes half the noise of an exploding chestnut in a fire? Nonsense. You might as well terrify boys with demons.

GRUMIO *[GRUMIO to himself]* Petruchio fears nothing.

GREMIO Listen, Hortensio. This man has fortunately arrived to better himself and to aid us.

HORTENSIO I promis'd we would be contributors
And bear his charge of wooing, whatsoe'er.

GREMIO And so we will, provided that he win her.

GRUMIO I would I were as sure of a good dinner.
[Enter TRANIO brave disguised as Lucentio, and BIONDELLO]

TRANIO Gentlemen, God save you! If I may be bold, 215
Tell me, I beseech you, which is the readiest way
To the house of Signior Baptista Minola?

BIONDELLO He that has the two fair daughters; is't he you mean?

TRANIO Even he, Biondello!

GREMIO Hark you, sir, you mean not her— 220

TRANIO Perhaps him and her, sir. What have you to do?

PETRUCHIO Not her that chides, sir, at any hand, I pray.

TRANIO I love no chiders, sir. Biondello, let's away.

LUCENTIO *[aside]* Well begun, Tranio.

HORTENSIO Sir, a word ere you go. 225
Are you a suitor to the maid you talk of, yea or no?

TRANIO And if I be, sir, is it any offence?

GREMIO No, if without more words you will get you hence.

TRANIO Why, sir, I pray, are not the streets as free
For me as for you?

GREMIO But so is not she. 230

TRANIO For what reason, I beseech you?

GREMIO For this reason, if you'll
know: That she's the choice love of Signior Gremio.

HORTENSIO That she's the chosen of Signior Hortensio.

HORTENSIO I promised that we would promote his courtship of Katherina, whatever happens.

GREMIO And we will, so long as he marries her.

GRUMIO I wish I were as certain of a good dinner as of Petruchio's marriage to Katherina. *[TRANIO enters disguised as Lucentio; the servant BIONDELLO follows.]*

TRANIO Gentlemen, may I ask your help? Could you give me directions to the house of Baptista Minola?

BIONDELLO Do you mean the man with two pretty daughters?

TRANIO That's the one, Biondello!

GREMIO Notice, maybe you didn't mean her—

TRANIO I meant Baptista and his daughter. Why do you ask?

PETRUCHIO You don't ask after the nagging daughter.

TRANIO I want no nags. Biondello, let's go.

LUCENTIO *[LUCENTIO to himself]* Good start, Tranio.

HORTENSIO Sir, could I speak with you before you depart? Are you courting the nagging daughter?

TRANIO If I choose to woo her, do I insult you?

GREMIO No, if you will leave without more conversation.

TRANIO Am I not free to walk the streets like you?

GREMIO She is not available.

TRANIO Why not?

GREMIO For this reason, if you must know: She is the girlfriend of Gremio.

HORTENSIO She's the girlfriend of Hortensio.

TRANIO Softly, my masters! If you be gentlemen,
Do me this right: hear me with patience. 240
Baptista is a noble gentleman
To whom my father is not all unknown,
And were his daughter fairer than she is,
She may more suitors have, and me for one.
Fair Leda's daughter had a thousand wooers. 245
Then well one more may fair Bianca have.
And so she shall. Lucentio shall make one,
Though Paris came in hope to speed alone.

GREMIO What! This gentleman will out-talk us all.

LUCENTIO Sir, give him head; I know he'll prove a jade. 250

PETRUCHIO Hortensio, to what end are all these words?

HORTENSIO Sir, let me be so bold as ask you,
Did you yet ever see Baptista's daughter?

TRANIO No, sir, but hear I do that he hath two,
The one as famous for a scolding tongue 255
As is the other for beauteous modesty.

PETRUCHIO Sir, sir, the first's for me; let her go by.

GREMIO Yea, leave that labour to great Hercules,
And let it be more than Alcides' twelve.

PETRUCHIO Sir, understand you this of me, in sooth: 260
The youngest daughter, whom you hearken for,
Her father keeps from all access of suitors
And will not promise her to any man
Until the elder sister first be wed.
The younger then is free, and not before. 265

TRANIO If it be so, sir, that you are the man
Must stead us all, and me amongst the rest,
And if you break the ice and do this feat,
Achieve the elder, set the younger free
For our access, whose hap shall be to have her 270
Will not so graceless be to be ingrate.

HORTENSIO Sir, you say well, and well you do conceive.
And since you do profess to be a suitor,
You must, as we do, gratify this gentleman,
To whom we all rest generally beholding. 275

TRANIO Simmer down, men! If you are gentlemen, be polite and listen to me. Baptista is a nobleman whom my father knows. If his daughter Bianca is fair, she could have many suitors, including me. Helen of Troy, the daughter of Jupiter and Leda, had a thousand suitors. Bianca can have one more. And so she shall. I will woo her despite the fact that Paris, the Trojan prince, expected no rivalry.

GREMIO This man will out-talk us all.

LUCENTIO Let him talk. He's a loser.

PETRUCHIO Hortensio, what is all this arguing about?

HORTENSIO Sir, have you seen Baptista's daughter Bianca?

TRANIO No, but I understand that he has two daughters—one is a notorious scold, and the other is known for modest beauty.

PETRUCHIO Sir, the first daughter is mine. Leave her alone.

GREMIO Leave that courtship to Hercules. Let the job be harder than Hercules's twelve labors.

PETRUCHIO Understand me. Baptista confines the younger daughter, Bianca, whom you want, and keeps all suitors away. He will not pledge her to anyone until the older sister Katherina marries. The younger girl is free to marry, but not until Katherina weds.

TRANIO If that is the case, Petruchio, you are the man to aid the rest of us. I would be grateful if you go first and win the older sister. You will release Bianca for the rest of us, whoever is lucky enough to win her. I will offer my thanks to you.

HORTENSIO You understand the situation and describe it clearly. If you are a suitor, you must please Petruchio, on whom we depend.

TRANIO Sir, I shall not be slack; in sign whereof,
Please you we may contrive this afternoon
And quaff carouses to our mistress' health,
And do as adversaries do in law,
Strive mightily, but eat and drink as friends. 280

GRUMIO, BIONDELLO O excellent motion! Fellows, let's be gone.

HORTENSIO The motion's good indeed, and be it so.
Petruchio, I shall be your ben venuto.
[Exeunt]

TRANIO I will get to my job. In proof, I offer to pay for drinks to Bianca this afternoon. Do the same as attorneys. Battle each other in court, but eat and drink like friends.

GRUMIO AND BIONDELLO Good idea! Pals, let's go.

HORTENSIO A good suggestion. I agree. Petruchio, I welcome you. *[The men depart.]*

ACT II, SCENE 1

Padua. A room in BAPTISTA'S house.

[Enter KATE and BIANCA with her hands bound]

BIANCA Good sister, wrong me not, nor wrong yourself,
To make a bondmaid and a slave of me.
That I disdain. But for these other gawds,
Unbind my hands, I'll pull them off myself,
Yea, all my raiment, to my petticoat, 5
Or what you will command me will I do,
So well I know my duty to my elders.

KATE Of all thy suitors here I charge thee tell
Whom thou lov'st best. See thou dissemble not.

BIANCA Believe me, sister, of all the men alive 10
I never yet beheld that special face
Which I could fancy more than any other.

KATE Minion, thou liest. Is't not Hortensio?

BIANCA If you affect him, sister, here I swear
I'll plead for you myself, but you shall have him. 15

KATE O, then belike you fancy riches more.
You will have Gremio to keep you fair.

BIANCA Is it for him you do envy me so?
Nay, then you jest, and now I well perceive
You have but jested with me all this while. 20
I prithee, sister Kate, untie my hands.

KATE If that be jest, then an the rest was so.
[Strikes her]
[Enter BAPTISTA]

BAPTISTA Why, how now, dame! Whence grows this insolence?
Bianca, stand aside. Poor girl, she weeps! *[Unties her hands]*
[To BIANCA] Go ply thy needle; meddle not with her. 25
[To KATE] For shame, thou hilding of a devilish spirit!
Why dost thou wrong her that did ne'er wrong thee?
When did she cross thee with a bitter word?

KATE Her silence flouts me, and I'll be reveng'd.
[Flies after BIANCA]

ACT II, SCENE 1

A room in the house of Baptista,
a wealthy man at Padua in north central Italy.

[KATE arrives with BIANCA, whose hands are tied.]

BIANCA Sister Kate, don't harm me or commit a sin by making me a prisoner and a slave. I hate being tied up. If you loosen my hands, I will give you my jewelry. I will give you my clothes down to my petticoat and do whatever you command. I know that I must obey my elders.

KATE Of all the men here, whom do you like best? Tell the truth.

BIANCA Of all the men in the world, I have never found one outstanding male.

KATE Hussy, you are lying. Don't you prefer Hortensio?

BIANCA If you want him for yourself, I swear you may have him.

KATE Perhaps you would rather have a rich man. You want Gremio to keep you in style.

BIANCA Are you jealous over Gremio? You are joking. You've been teasing me all this time. Please, Kate, untie me.

KATE If that is a joke, then the rest was true. *[KATE slaps BIANCA.] [BAPTISTA enters.]*

BAPTISTA What are you doing, missy! How dare you be so impertinent? Bianca, stand away from her. Poor child, she is crying! *[Baptista unties Bianca's hands.] [Baptista to Bianca]* Go do your needlework. Don't bother Katherina. *[Baptista to Kate]* Shame on you, you wretch with a demon's spirit! Why do you harass her when she does no harm to you? When did she annoy you with a bitter word?

KATE Her silence irks me. I'll punish her for it. *[KATHERINA races after BIANCA.]*

BAPTISTA What, in my sight? Bianca, get thee in. 30
[Exit BIANCA]

KATE What, will you not suffer me? Nay, now I see
She is your treasure, she must have a husband,
I must dance bare-foot on her wedding-day
And, for your love to her, lead apes in hell.
Talk not to me: I will go sit and weep 35
Till I can find occasion of revenge.
[Exit]

BAPTISTA Was ever gentleman thus griev'd as I?
But who comes here?
[Enter GREMIO, LUCENTIO (disguised as Cambio) in the habit of a mean man; PETRUCHIO, with HORTENSIO (disguised as Litio); and TRANIO (disguised as Lucentio), with his boy (BIONDELLO), bearing a lute and books]

GREMIO Good morrow, neighbour Baptista.

BAPTISTA Good morrow, neighbour Gremio. God save you, gentlemen! 40

PETRUCHIO And you, good sir! Pray, have you not a daughter
Call'd Katherina, fair and virtuous?

BAPTISTA I have a daughter, sir, call'd Katherina.

GREMIO You are too blunt. Go to it orderly.

PETRUCHIO You wrong me, Signior Gremio. Give me leave. 45
I am a gentleman of Verona, sir,
That hearing of her beauty and her wit,
Her affability and bashful modesty,
Her wondrous qualities and mild behaviour,
Am bold to show myself a forward guest 50
Within your house, to make mine eye the witness
Of that report which I so oft have heard.
And, for an entrance to my entertainment,
I do present you with a man of mine,
[Presents HORTENSIO, disguised as Litio]
Cunning in music and the mathematics, 55
To instruct her fully in those sciences,
Whereof I know she is not ignorant.
Accept of him, or else you do me wrong.
His name is Litio, born in Mantua.

BAPTISTA You fight under my nose? Bianca hurry away. *[BIANCA departs]*

KATE Won't you take my side? You obviously treasure her. You want her to wed. I will be humiliated on her wedding date as the old maid. Because you love her, I must lead apes in hell. Don't talk to me. I will go cry until I find a way to retaliate. *[KATHERINA goes out.]*

BAPTISTA Was there ever a more troubled father than I? Who is this? *[GREMIO enters with LUCENTIO, who is disguised as Cambio, a commoner. PETRUCHIO enters with HORTENSIO disguised as Litio. TRANIO, disguised as Lucentio, enters with his servant BIONDELLO, who carries a lute and books.]*

GREMIO Good morning, neighbor Baptista.

BAPTISTA Good morning, Gremio. Greetings, gentlemen!

PETRUCHIO Greetings to you, sir! Do you have a beautiful, pure daughter called Katherina?

BAPTISTA I have a daughter named Katherina.

GREMIO You are too curt. Request her properly.

PETRUCHIO You misunderstand me, Gremio. Let me explain. I come from Verona, sir. I have heard of her beauty and intelligence, her friendliness and shy modesty, her wonderful talents and gentleness. I have come as a guest at your home to see for myself if she is equal to her description. In exchange for allowing me to enter your residence, I give you this man. *[PETRUCHIO presents HORTENSIO, who is disguised as Litio.]* He is skilled in music and math. He will teach her subjects that she already knows. Receive him or you insult me. He is Litio of Mantua.

BAPTISTA You're welcome, sir, and he for your good sake. 60
But for my daughter Katherine, this I know,
She is not for your turn, the more my grief.

PETRUCHIO I see you do not mean to part with her;
Or else you like not of my company.

BAPTISTA Mistake me not. I speak but as I find. 65
Whence are you, sir? What may I call your name?

PETRUCHIO Petruchio is my name. Antonio's son,
A man well known throughout all Italy.

BAPTISTA I know him well. You are welcome for his sake.

GREMIO Saving your tale, Petruchio, I pray let us that are poor 70
petitioners speak too. Backare, you are marvelous forward.

PETRUCHIO O, pardon me, Signior Gremio, I would fain be doing.

GREMIO I doubt it not, sir. But you will curse your wooing.
[To BAPTISTA] Neighbour, this is a gift very grateful, I am 75
sure of it. To express the like kindness, myself, that
have been more kindly beholding to you than any, freely give
unto you this young scholar, *[Presents LUCENTIO, disguised as Cambio]* that hath been long studying at Rheims, as cunning
in Greek, Latin, and other languages, 80
as the other in music and mathematics. His name is
Cambio. Pray accept his service.

BAPTISTA A thousand thanks, Signior Gremio. Welcome, good Cambio.
[To TRANIO as Lucentio] But, gentle sir, methinks you walk
like a stranger. May I be so bold to know the 85
cause of your coming?

BAPTISTA You are welcome, Petruchio. I also welcome Litio as your gift. As for my daughter Katherina, I must admit that she does not fit the description. It grieves me.

PETRUCHIO I think you don't want to lose her. Or you do not approve of me as a suitor.

BAPTISTA You misunderstand. I must tell you the truth. Where do you come from? What is your name?

PETRUCHIO I am Petruchio, son of Antonio, a man known all over Italy.

BAPTISTA I know him well. Antonio's son is very welcome.

GREMIO Excuse me for interrupting, Petruchio. Let the rest of us have a word with Baptista. Stand back. You are terribly pushy.

PETRUCHIO Pardon me, Gremio. I am eager to state my business.

GREMIO I know you are eager, sir. But you will ruin your chance to court her. *[GREMIO to BAPTISTA]* Neighbor, I know that this is a welcome gift. To express my friendship and gratitude, I give you this young teacher. *[Gremio presents Lucentio, who is disguised as Cambio.]* He has studied long at Rheims in France. He is educated in Greek, Latin, and other languages and in music and math. His name is Cambio. Please accept him as a tutor.

BAPTISTA Many thanks, Gremio. Welcome, Cambio. *[BAPTISTA speaks to TRANIO, who is disguised as Lucentio*] Sir, you walk like a foreigner. May I ask why you came?

TRANIO Pardon me, sir, the boldness is mine own,
That being a stranger in this city here
Do make myself a suitor to your daughter,
Unto Bianca, fair and virtuous. 90
Nor is your firm resolve unknown to me,
In the preferment of the eldest sister.
This liberty is all that I request,
That, upon knowledge of my parentage,
I may have welcome 'mongst the rest that woo 95
And free access and favour as the rest.
And, toward the education of your daughters,
I here bestow a simple instrument
And this small packet of Greek and Latin books.
[BIONDELLO offers the gifts to BAPTISTA.]
If you accept them, then their worth is great. 100

BAPTISTA Lucentio is your name. Of whence, I pray?

TRANIO Of Pisa, sir; son to Vincentio.

BAPTISTA A mighty man of Pisa. By report
I know him well. You are very welcome, sir.
[To HORTENSIO as Litio] Take you the lute, 105
[To LUCENTIO as Cambio] and you the set of books.
You shall go see your pupils presently.
Holla, within!
[Enter a SERVANT]
Sirrah, lead these gentlemen
To my two daughters, and tell them both 110
These are their tutors. Bid them use them well.
[Exit SERVANT, with HORTENSIO, LUCENTIO, and BIONDELLO]
We will go walk a little in the orchard,
And then to dinner. You are passing welcome,
And so I pray you all to think yourselves.

PETRUCHIO Signior Baptista, my business asketh haste, 115
And every day I cannot come to woo.
You knew my father well, and in him me,
Left solely heir to all his lands and goods,
Which I have bettered rather than decreas'd.
Then tell me, if I get your daughter's love, 120
What dowry shall I have with her to wife?

BAPTISTA After my death, the one half of my lands,
And in possession twenty thousand crowns.

TRANIO Pardon my boldness, sir. I am a newcomer to Padua. I come to court your daughter, the lovely and pure Bianca. I know that you intend to arrange the older sister's marriage first. I ask your permission. Because you know my parents, I want to join the others in courting Bianca freely and openly. To the training of your daughters, I offer a lute and a stack of Greek and Latin books. *[BIONDELLO extends the gifts to BAPTISTA.]* If you accept them, then they are worthy gifts.

BAPTISTA I see written in the books that your name is Lucentio. Where do you come from?

TRANIO From Pisa, sir. I am Vincentio's son.

BAPTISTA Vincentio is an influential Pisan. I know his reputation. I welcome you, sir. *[BAPTISTA to HORTENSIO disguised as Litio]* You take the lute. *[BAPTISTA to LUCENTIO disguised as Cambio]* And you take the language books. You shall meet your students immediately. Houseboy! *[A SERVANT enters.]* Escort these gentlemen to my daughters. Tell Bianca and Katherina that these men are tutors. Encourage the girls to study well. *[The SERVANT departs with HORTENSIO, LUCENTIO, and BIONDELLO.]* Let's walk in the garden before dinner. I want you all to make yourselves at home.

PETRUCHIO Baptista, I have little time for this courtship. I can't come here every day. You knew my father well and, through him, you know me. I inherited all his property and wealth, which I have increased. If I win Katherina's love, what dowry do you offer her husband?

BAPTISTA After I die, she inherits half my property. Her husband receives immediately ten thousand dollars.

PETRUCHIO And, for that dowry, I'll assure her of
Her widowhood, be it that she survive me, 125
In all my lands and leases whatsoever.
Let specialities be therefore drawn between us,
That covenants may be kept on either hand.

BAPTISTA Ay, when the special thing is well obtain'd,
That is, her love, for that is all in all. 130

PETRUCHIO Why, that is nothing. For I tell you, father,
I am as peremptory as she proud-minded;
And where two raging fires meet together,
They do consume the thing that feeds their fury.
Though little fire grows great with little wind, 135
Yet extreme gusts will blow out fire and all.
So I to her and so she yields to me,
For I am rough and woo not like a babe.

BAPTISTA Well mayst thou woo, and happy be thy speed!
But be thou arm'd for some unhappy words. 140

PETRUCHIO Ay, to the proof, as mountains are for winds,
That shakes not, though they blow perpetually.
[Enter HORTENSIO, as Litio, with his head broke]

BAPTISTA How now, my friend! Why dost thou look so pale?

HORTENSIO For fear, I promise you, if I look pale.

BAPTISTA What, will my daughter prove a good musician? 145

HORTENSIO I think she'll sooner prove a soldier.
Iron may hold with her, but never lutes.

BAPTISTA Why, then thou canst not break her to the lute?

HORTENSIO Why, no, for she hath broke the lute to me.
I did but tell her she mistook her frets, 150
And bow'd her hand to teach her fingering.
When, with a most impatient devilish spirit,
"Frets, call you these?" quoth she. "I'll fume with them!"
And with that word she struck me on the head,
And through the instrument my pate made way, 155
And there I stood amazèd for a while,
As on a pillory, looking through the lute,
While she did call me "rascal fiddler,"
And "twangling Jack," with twenty such vile terms,
As she had studied to misuse me so. 160

PETRUCHIO I will guarantee her that amount in property and rents if I die before her. Let's draw up a contract and each keep a copy.

BAPTISTA First and most important, you must win her love.

PETRUCHIO That is no problem. I promise that I am as determined as she is proud. When two flames meet, they burn up the fuel that feeds them. Although small fires flare up in wind, gales will blow out the flame. I am like a gale to her. She will accept me. I am hearty. I don't court her like a boy.

BAPTISTA I wish you well in your swift courtship! Be ready for some foul retorts from her.

PETRUCHIO I am like a mountain that remains unmoved, even against constant wind. *[HORTENSIO disguised as Litio enters with a wounded head.]*

BAPTISTA What happened? Why are you so pale?

HORTENSIO I am pale from fear.

BAPTISTA Will my daughter become a good lute player?

HORTENSIO She would make a better soldier. She is better at iron weapons than at lutes.

BAPTISTA You mean you can't teach her to play the lute?

HORTENSIO No. She broke the lute over my head. I told her she placed her fingers wrong. I bent her hand to teach her fingering. Like a demon, she said, "Do you call these frets? I'll rage at them!" She hit me on the head. My head broke through the lute. I was temporarily dazed. I peered through the lute as though I were pilloried. She called me "rascal fiddler" and "twanging Jack." She had a list of twenty insults that she had prepared to yell at me.

PETRUCHIO Now, by the world, it is a lusty wench!
I love her ten times more than e'er I did.
O, how I long to have some chat with her!

BAPTISTA *[To HORTENSIO, as LITIO]*
Well, go with me, and be not so discomfited.
Proceed in practice with my younger daughter. 165
She's apt to learn, and thankful for good turns.
Signior Petruchio, will you go with us,
Or shall I send my daughter Kate to you?

PETRUCHIO I pray you do. I will attend her here.
[Exeunt all but PETRUCHIO]
And woo her with some spirit when she comes. 170
Say that she rail, why, then I'll tell her plain
She sings as sweetly as a nightingale.
Say that she frown, I'll say she looks as clear
As morning roses newly wash'd with dew.
Say she be mute, and will not speak a word, 175
Then I'll commend her volubility
And say she uttereth piercing eloquence.
If she do bid me pack, I'll give her thanks
As though she bid me stay by her a week.
If she deny to wed, I'll crave the day 180
When I shall ask the banns, and when be married.
But here she comes, and now, Petruchio, speak.
[Enter KATE]
Good morrow, Kate, for that's your name, I hear.

KATE Well have you heard, but something hard of hearing.
They call me Katherina that do talk of me. 185

PETRUCHIO You lie, in faith, for you are call'd plain Kate,
And bonny Kate, and sometimes Kate the curst.
But Kate, the prettiest Kate in Christendom,
Kate of Kate Hall, my super-dainty Kate,
For dainties are all Kates: and therefore, Kate, 190
Take this of me, Kate of my consolation:
Hearing thy mildness prais'd in every town,
Thy virtues spoke of, and thy beauty sounded
Yet not so deeply as to thee belongs,
Myself am mov'd to woo thee for my wife. 195

KATE Mov'd! In good time! Let him that mov'd you hither
Remove you hence. I knew you at the first
You were a movable.

PETRUCHIO Why, what's a movable?

PETRUCHIO Truly, Katherina is a hearty girl! I love her ten times more than I did when I arrived. I would love to chat with her!

BAPTISTA *[BAPTISTA to HORTENSIO disguised as Litio]* Come with me and don't be disturbed. Continue tutoring my younger daughter. She is a quick learner and grateful for your kindness. Petruchio, will you go with us or shall I sent Kate to you?

PETRUCHIO Send her here. I will wait for her. *[All depart except PETRUCHIO.]* I will briskly court her when she arrives. If she rants, I will say that her voice is like a nightingale. If she frowns, I will say that she is as pleasant as roses washed in morning dew. If she is silent, I will compliment her conversation as eloquent. If she orders me to leave, I will thank her for inviting me to stay for a week. If she refuses to marry me, I will anticipate the day when I post the announcement of our wedding. Here she comes. Petruchio, speak to her. *[KATE enters.]* Good morning, Kate. I understand that is your name.

KATE Your heard right, but you are a little deaf. People speak of me as Katherina.

PETRUCHIO You lie. People call you plain Kate and pretty Kate and sometimes Kate the cursed. But you are Kate, the prettiest Kate in all Christian lands, Kate of Kate Hall, my extra-delicate Kate, for all delicacies are Kates. Listen to me, Kate, my pleasure. I have heard your gentleness praised in every town. People speak of your goodness and your beauty, but they didn't praise you enough. I came to propose marriage to you.

KATE Are you deranged? Immediately, let whatever brought you here take you away. I knew at first sight you were unstable.

PETRUCHIO What thing is movable?

KATE	A joint-stool.	200
PETRUCHIO	Thou hast hit it. Come, sit on me.	
KATE	Asses are made to bear, and so are you.	
PETRUCHIO	Women are made to bear, and so are you.	
KATE	No such jade as you, if me you mean.	
PETRUCHIO	Alas, good Kate, I will not burden thee, For, knowing thee to be but young and light.	205
KATE	Too light for such a swain as you to catch; And yet as heavy as my weight should be.	
PETRUCHIO	Should be! Should buzz!	
KATE	Well ta'en, and like a buzzard.	210
PETRUCHIO	O, slow-wing'd turtle, shall a buzzard take thee?	
KATE	Ay, for a turtle, as he takes a buzzard.	
PETRUCHIO	Come, come, you wasp! I' faith, you are too angry.	
KATE	If I be waspish, best beware my sting.	
PETRUCHIO	My remedy is then to pluck it out.	215
KATE	Ay, if the fool could find it where it lies.	
PETRUCHIO	Who knows not where a wasp does wear his sting? In his tail.	
KATE	In his tongue.	
PETRUCHIO	Whose tongue?	220
KATE	Yours, if you talk of tales, and so farewell.	
PETRUCHIO	What, with my tongue in your tail? Nay, come again, Good Kate. I am a gentleman.	
KATE	That I'll try. *[She strikes him.]*	
PETRUCHIO	I swear I'll cuff you if you strike again.	225
KATE	So may you lose your arms. If you strike me, you are no gentleman, And if no gentleman, why then no arms.	
PETRUCHIO	A herald, Kate? O! put me in thy books.	
KATE	What is your crest? A coxcomb?	230

KATE	A folding stool.
PETRUCHIO	Exactly. Come sit on me.
KATE	Donkeys are meant for carrying people. That makes you an ass.
PETRUCHIO	Women are made to bear children and so are you.
KATE	I would have no jerk like you, if you mean to marry me.
PETRUCHIO	I won't upset you, because I know you are young and light-hearted.
KATE	I am too light for you to catch. I am as heavy as a woman should be.
PETRUCHIO	Should be! You should buzz like a bee!
KATE	That's a good joke. Buzz like a buzzard.
PETRUCHIO	Slow-flying turtledove, will a buzzard catch you?
KATE	Yes, a turtledove that can catch a buzzard.
PETRUCHIO	Come, you wasp! You are too angry.
KATE	If I am a wasp, watch out for my stinger.
PETRUCHIO	I will pull it out.
KATE	If you could find my stinger.
PETRUCHIO	Everybody knows where the stinger is—in the wasp's tail.
KATE	In his tongue.
PETRUCHIO	Whose tongue?
KATE	Your tongue, which tells lies. Goodbye.
PETRUCHIO	With my tongue in your tail! No, come back, Kate. I am a gentleman.
KATE	This is my answer. *[KATE slaps PETRUCHIO.]*
PETRUCHIO	If you hit me again, I'll smack you.
KATE	If you hit women, you destroy your honorable coat of arms. If you hit me, you are no gentleman. If you are not a gentleman, you have no honor.
PETRUCHIO	Are you a messenger, Kate? Record me in your favor.
KATE	What is your family crest? A rooster's comb?

PETRUCHIO A combless cock, so Kate will be my hen.

KATE No cock of mine. You crow too like a craven.

PETRUCHIO Nay, come, Kate, come. You must not look so sour.

KATE It is my fashion when I see a crab.

PETRUCHIO Why, here's no crab, and therefore look not sour. 235

KATE There is, there is.

PETRUCHIO Then show it me.

KATE Had I a glass I would.

PETRUCHIO What, you mean my face?

KATE Well aim'd of such a young one. 240

PETRUCHIO Now, by Saint George, I am too young for you.

KATE Yet you are wither'd.

PETRUCHIO 'Tis with cares.

KATE I care not.

PETRUCHIO Nay, hear you, Kate: in sooth, you 'scape not so. 245

KATE I chafe you if I tarry. Let me go.

PETRUCHIO No, not a whit. I find you passing gentle.
'Twas told me you were rough, and coy, and sullen,
And now I find report a very liar.
For thou art pleasant, gamesome, passing courteous, 250
But slow in speech, yet sweet as springtime flowers.
Thou canst not frown, thou canst not look askance,
Nor bite the lip as angry wenches will,
Nor hast thou pleasure to be cross in talk.
But thou with mildness entertain'st thy wooers, 255
With gentle conference, soft and affable.
Why does the world report that Kate doth limp?
O sland'rous world! Kate like the hazeltwig
Is straight and slender, and as brown in hue
As hazelnuts, and sweeter than the kernels. 260
O, let me see thee walk! Thou dost not halt.

KATE Go, fool, and whom thou keep'st command.

PETRUCHIO I will be a humble rooster if Kate will be my hen.

KATE I refuse such a rooster. You crow like a coward.

PETRUCHIO Please, Kate. Don't be so sour-faced.

KATE That is what I do when I see a crabapple.

PETRUCHIO I'm not a crabapple. Don't frown at me.

KATE You are a crabapple.

PETRUCHIO Prove it.

KATE If I had a mirror, I would.

PETRUCHIO You would show me my face?

KATE You are quick for so young a man.

PETRUCHIO By Saint George the dragon slayer, I am too young for you.

KATE But you are wrinkled.

PETRUCHIO With worry.

KATE I don't care.

PETRUCHIO Listen to yourself, Kate. You can't slip away from me.

KATE I will annoy you if I stay. Let me go.

PETRUCHIO I won't. You are quite gentle. I heard that you were harsh, dismissive, and pouty. That report is a lie. You are pleasant, sporty, mannerly, shy in conversation, and sweet as spring blossoms. You don't frown or look scornful. You don't bite your lip in anger. You don't enjoy being contrary. You entertain your boyfriends with gentle conversation, soft and friendly. Why do people say that Kate is crippled? Oh, liars! Kate is as straight and slender as a hazel twig and as tan and sweet as hazelnuts. Let me see your walk! You are not crippled.

KATE Go away, idiot, and command your servants.

PETRUCHIO Did ever Dian so become a grove
As Kate this chamber with her princely gait?
O! be thou Dian, and let her be Kate, 265
And then let Kate be chaste, and Dian sportful!

KATE Where did you study all this goodly speech?

PETRUCHIO It is extempore, from my motherwit.

KATE A witty mother, witless else her son.

PETRUCHIO Am I not wise? 270

KATE Yes, keep you warm.

PETRUCHIO Marry, so I mean, sweet Katherina, in thy bed.
And therefore, setting all this chat aside,
Thus in plain terms: your father hath consented
That you shall be my wife, your dowry 'greed on, 275
And, will you, nill you, I will marry you.
Now, Kate, I am a husband for your turn,
For by this light, whereby I see thy beauty,
Thy beauty that doth make me like thee well,
Thou must be married to no man but me. 280
For I am he am born to tame you, Kate,
And bring you from a wild Kate to a Kate
Conformable as other household Kates.
[Enter BAPTISTA, GREMIO, TRANIO (as Lucentio)]
Here comes your father. Never make denial.
I must and will have Katherine to my wife. 285

BAPTISTA Now, Signior Petruchio, how speed you with my daughter?

PETRUCHIO How but well, sir? How but well?
It were impossible I should speed amiss.

BAPTISTA Why, how now, daughter Katherina? In your dumps?

KATE Call you me daughter? Now I promise you 290
You have show'd a tender fatherly regard,
To wish me wed to one half lunatic,
A madcap ruffian and a swearing Jack,
That thinks with oaths to face the matter out.

PETRUCHIO Did the goddess Diana ever walk so beautifully in the woods as Kate walks in this room? Take her place as Diana and let her be Kate. Let Kate be pure and Diana competitive!

KATE Where did you study these speeches?

PETRUCHIO It is unrehearsed, my native intelligence.

KATE A witty mother who had a simplewitted son.

PETRUCHIO Am I not wise?

KATE Yes, you are witty enough to warm yourself.

PETRUCHIO Sweet Katherina, I intend to warm myself in your bed. Let's speak plain. Your father has agreed that I shall marry you. I agreed to your dowry. Like it or not, I will wed you. I am a suitable mate for you. When I see you in this light, your beauty pleases me. You shall marry no one but me. I was meant to tame you, Kate. I will reduce you from a wild Kate to an obedient Kate like other wives. *[BAPTISTA enters with GREMIO and with TRANIO disguised as Lucentio.]* Here comes your father. Don't reject me. I must and will marry Katherina.

BAPTISTA Petruchio, have you made progress with my daughter?

PETRUCHIO Of course! Of course! It is impossible to fail.

BAPTISTA How are you, Katherina! Are you grumpy?

KATE Do you call me your daughter? You have displayed your fatherly tenderness by wanting me to marry a halfwit. He's a zany rascal, a foul-mouthed rowdy who courts me with swearing.

PETRUCHIO Father, 'tis thus: yourself and all the world 295
That talk'd of her have talk'd amiss of her.
If she be curst, it is for policy,
For she's not froward, but modest as the dove;
She is not hot, but temperate as the morn.
For patience she will prove a second Grissel, 300
And Roman Lucrece for her chastity.
And to conclude, we have 'greed so well together
That upon Sunday is the wedding day.

KATE I'll see thee hang'd on Sunday first.

GREMIO Hark, Petruchio, she says she'll see thee hang'd first. 305

TRANIO Is this your speeding? Nay, then, goodnight our part!

PETRUCHIO Be patient, gentlemen. I choose her for myself.
If she and I be pleas'd, what's that to you?
'Tis bargain'd 'twixt us twain, being alone,
That she shall still be curst in company. 310
I tell you, 'tis incredible to believe
How much she loves me. O, the kindest Kate!
She hung about my neck, and kiss on kiss
She vied so fast, protesting oath on oath,
That in a twink she won me to her love. 315
O, you are novices! 'Tis a world to see
How tame, when men and women are alone,
A meacock wretch can make the curstest shrew.
Give me thy hand, Kate. I will unto Venice
To buy apparel 'gainst the wedding-day. 320
Provide the feast, father, and bid the guests.
I will be sure my Katherine shall be fine.

BAPTISTA I know not what to say, but give me your hands.
God send you joy, Petruchio! 'Tis a match.

GREMIO, TRANIO Amen, say we. We will be witnesses. 325

PETRUCHIO Father, and wife, and gentlemen, adieu.
I will to Venice; Sunday comes apace.
We will have rings, and things, and fine array,
And kiss me, Kate. We will be married o' Sunday.
[Exeunt PETRUCHIO and KATE, severally]

GREMIO Was ever match clapp'd up so suddenly? 330

BAPTISTA Faith, gentlemen, now I play a merchant's part
And venture madly on a desperate mart.

PETRUCHIO Father Baptista, she's right. Your description and rumors about her are false. If she is foul-tempered, it is for a reason. She is not pushy, but gentle as a dove. She is not angry, but cool as the morning. She is as patient as Griselda, the submissive wife of fable. She is as pure as the Roman Lucretia, who killed herself after a king shamed her. We have agreed to marry on Sunday.

KATE May you hang on Sunday.

GREMIO Petruchio, she would rather see you executed.

TRANIO Is this the best you can do? You've ruined our hopes for Bianca!

PETRUCHIO Don't be so hasty, gentlemen. I choose her for my wife. If we please each other, what do you care? It is a private bargain. She is still foul-tempered in public. You won't believe how much she loves me. She is the kindest Kate! She embraced my neck and kissed me often with vows of love. In a twinkling, she won my love. You men are beginners! It is marvelous how, in private, a timid man can court a raging nag. Give me your hand, Kate. I am going east to Venice to buy garments for our wedding. Father, order a feast and invite the guests. I know that Katherina agrees.

BAPTISTA I don't know what to say, but shake my hand. God bless you, Petruchio! I accept this match.

GREMIO AND TRANIO We agree. We will be witnesses to this agreement.

PETRUCHIO Father-in-law and wife and gentlemen, God be with you. I am going to Venice. It will soon be Sunday. We will have rings and adornments and elegant clothes. Kiss me, Kate. We will marry on Sunday. *[PETRUCHIO and KATE depart in opposite directions.]*

GREMIO Was there ever so rapid a courtship?

BAPTISTA Now I must be the seller and hurry to complete my part of the bargain.

TRANIO 'Twas a commodity lay fretting by you.
'Twill bring you gain, or perish on the seas.

BAPTISTA The gain I seek is quiet in the match. 335

GREMIO No doubt but he hath got a quiet catch.
But now, Baptista, to your younger daughter.
Now is the day we long have looked for.
I am your neighbour and was suitor first.

TRANIO And I am one that love Bianca more 340
Than words can witness or your thoughts can guess.

GREMIO Youngling, thou canst not love so dear as I.

TRANIO Greybeard, thy love doth freeze.

GREMIO But thine doth fry.
Skipper, stand back. 'Tis age that nourisheth. 345

TRANIO But youth in ladies' eyes that flourisheth.

BAPTISTA Content you, gentlemen. I will compound this strife.
'Tis deeds must win the prize, and he of both
That can assure my daughter greatest dower
Shall have my Bianca's love. 350
Say, Signior Gremio, what can you assure her?

GREMIO First, as you know, my house within the city
Is richly furnished with plate and gold,
Basins and ewers to lave her dainty hands;
My hangings all of Tyrian tapestry; 355
In ivory coffers I have stuff'd my crowns,
In cypress chests my arras counterpoints,
Costly apparel, tents, and canopies,
Fine linen, Turkey cushions boss'd with pearl,
Valance of Venice gold in needlework, 360
Pewter and brass, and all things that belong
To house or housekeeping. Then, at my farm
I have a hundred milch-kine to the pail,
Six score fat oxen standing in my stalls,
And all things answerable to this portion. 365
Myself am struck in years, I must confess;
And if I die tomorrow this is hers,
If whilst I live she will be only mine.

TRANIO She was wasted goods in your store. You will profit from this bargain or drown in the ocean.

BAPTISTA I seek only a quiet match.

GREMIO Petruchio has caught a quiet fish. Baptista, move on to the engagement of your younger daughter. We suitors have longed for a chance to court her. I am your neighbor and the first to woo Bianca.

TRANIO I love Bianca more than words can say or thoughts can guess.

GREMIO Young sprout, you can't love her as dearly as I do.

TRANIO Old man, your love is cold.

GREMIO Yours is too hot. Upstart, give up. Maturity is more nourishing to love.

TRANIO But ladies prefer youth.

BAPTISTA Stop quarreling, gentlemen. I will settle this argument. Action will end this competition. The man who offers the most money shall have Bianca. Gremio, what do you guarantee her?

GREMIO You know that my house in Padua is furnished in silver and gold. I have bowls and pitchers for washing her delicate hands. My walls display expensive purple hangings. I have ivory chests full of gold coins. Cypress boxes hold embroidered bedspreads. I own expensive garments, ceiling draperies, and bed canopies, fine linens, and Turkish pillows stitched with pearls. I have window curtains embroidered in Venetian gold, pewter and brass, and all the equipment for housekeeping. My farm has a hundred productive milk cows. One hundred and twenty fat oxen occupy the stalls in my barn. Everything I own is of the same quality. I confess that I am old. If I die tomorrow, she will inherit all. While I live, she will be only mine.

TRANIO That 'only' came well in. *[To BAPTISTA]* Sir, list to me:
I am my father's heir and only son. 370
If I may have your daughter to my wife,
I'll leave her houses three or four as good,
Within rich Pisa's walls, as any one
Old Signior Gremio has in Padua,
Besides two thousand ducats by the year 375
Of fruitful land, all which shall be her jointure.
What, have I pinch'd you, Signior Gremio?

GREMIO Two thousand ducats by the year of land?
[aside] My land amounts not to so much in all.
That she shall have, besides an argosy 380
That now is lying in Marseilles' road.
[To TRANIO] What, have I chok'd you with an argosy?

TRANIO Gremio, 'tis known my father hath no less
Than three great argosies, besides two galliasses
And twelve tight galleys. These I will assure her, 385
And twice as much, whate'er thou offer'st next.

GREMIO Nay, I have offer'd all. I have no more,
And she can have no more than all I have.
[To BAPTISTA] If you like me, she shall have me and mine.

TRANIO Why, then, the maid is mine from all the world, 390
By your firm promise. Gremio is outvied.

BAPTISTA I must confess your offer is the best,
And, let your father make her the assurance,
She is your own; else, you must pardon me.
If you should die before him, where's her dower? 395

TRANIO That's but a cavil. He is old, I young.

GREMIO And may not young men die as well as old?

BAPTISTA Well, gentlemen,
I am thus resolv'd: On Sunday next, you know,
My daughter Katherina is to be married. 400
[To TRANIO] Now, on the Sunday following, shall Bianca
Be bride to you, if you make this assurance.
If not, to Signior Gremio.
And so I take my leave, and thank you both.

TRANIO "Only" is a good place to stop. *[TRANIO to BAPTISTA]* Sir, listen to me. I am my father's heir and only son. If I marry your daughter, I will leave her three or four houses in Pisa as worthy as any one that Gremio owns in Padua. Also, I offer her $7,000 a year profit from productive land. Have I squelched you, Gremio?

GREMIO You have $7,000 a year in profits from your land? *[GREMIO to himself]* My land doesn't earn that much. I will also give her a merchant ship that is anchored in Marseilles, France. *[GREMIO to TRANIO]* Did I outbid you with a ship?

TRANIO Gremio, it is no secret that my father owns three merchant vessels, two large sailing ships, and twelve galleys. I will pledge them to Bianca and twice any amount that Gremio can offer.

GREMIO That is all I have to offer. I have nothing else. She can have all that I own. *[GREMIO to BAPTISTA]* If you choose me, she will have me and all my goods.

TRANIO According to Baptista, I win Bianca. I defeated Gremio.

BAPTISTA I agree that you made the best offer. If your father guarantees your offer, Bianca is yours. There is one more issue. If you die before your father, what will she inherit?

TRANIO That is a senseless quibble. He is old; I am young.

GREMIO Can't young men die the same as old men?

BAPTISTA Gentlemen, I have made up my mind. My daughter Katherina will marry next Sunday. *[BAPTISTA to TRANIO]* The following Sunday, you will wed Bianca if you guarantee your offer. If you fail, Gremio will marry her. That is all I have to say. Thank you both.

GREMIO Adieu, good neighbour. 405
[Exit BAPTISTA]
Now, I fear thee not.
Sirrah young gamester, your father were a fool
To give thee all and in his waning age
Set foot under thy table. Tut, a toy!
An old Italian fox is not so kind, my boy. 410
[Exit GREMIO]

TRANIO A vengeance on your crafty wither'd hide!
Yet I have fac'd it with a card of ten.
'Tis in my head to do my master good.
I see no reason but suppos'd Lucentio
Must get a father, call'd 'suppos'd Vincentio'; 415
And that's a wonder. Fathers commonly
Do get their children. But in this case of wooing,
A child shall get a sire, if I fail not of my cunning.
[Exit]

GREMIO God be with you, neighbor. *[BAPTISTA departs.]* I don't fear you. Young gambler, your father would be unwise to give you an inheritance now and to live under your roof. What nonsense! A foxy old Italian is not so foolish, my boy. *[GREMIO departs.]*

TRANIO Curses on your sly wrinkled hide! I have bluffed with only a low card. I plan to win for my master. It will be a miracle if Lucentio can produce a father, the aforementioned Vincentio. Usually, fathers beget children. In this case, if my plan works, the son will beget a father. *[TRANIO departs.]*

ACT III, SCENE 1

Padua. A room in BAPTISTA'S house.

[Enter LUCENTIO (as Cambio), HORTENSIO (as Litio), and BIANCA]

LUCENTIO Fiddler, forbear. You grow too forward, sir.
Have you so soon forgot the entertainment
Her sister Katherina welcome'd you withal?

HORTENSIO But, wrangling pedant, this is
The patroness of heavenly harmony. 5
Then give me leave to have prerogative,
And when in music we have spent an hour,
Your lecture shall have leisure for as much.

LUCENTIO Preposterous ass, that never read so far
To know the cause why music was ordain'd! 10
Was it not to refresh the mind of man
After his studies or his usual pain?
Then give me leave to read philosophy,
And, while I pause, serve in your harmony.

HORTENSIO Sirrah, I will not bear these braves of thine. 15

BIANCA Why, gentlemen, you do me double wrong
To strive for that which resteth in my choice.
I am no breeching scholar in the schools.
I'll not be tied to hours nor 'pointed times,
But learn my lessons as I please myself. 20
And, to cut off all strife, here sit we down.
[To HORTENSIO] Take you your instrument,
play you the whiles;
His lecture will be done ere you have tun'd.

HORTENSIO You'll leave his lecture when I am in tune?

LUCENTIO That will be never. Tune your instrument. 25
[HORTENSIO stands aside, tuning his lute.]

BIANCA Where left we last?

LUCENTIO Here, madam:
[Opens the book to show BIANCA and reads]
'Hic ibat Simois; hic est Sigeia tellus,
Hic steterat Priami regia celsa senis.

ACT III, SCENE 1

A room in the house of Baptista,
a wealthy man at Padua in north central Italy.

[LUCENTIO disguised as Cambio and HORTENSIO disguised as Litio enter with BIANCA.]

LUCENTIO Fiddle teacher, halt. You are too pushy. Have you forgotten how Katherina welcomed you with a lute over your head?

HORTENSIO You quarrelsome bore, Bianca is the benefactor of God's harmony. Give me first place. After we spend an hour studying music, you may have an hour for your lesson.

LUCENTIO Presumptuous twirp, haven't you read why music was invented! It's purpose is to refresh the mind after lessons or after hardship. Let me read philosophy to her. When I stop, you teach her harmony.

HORTENSIO I won't tolerate your rudeness.

BIANCA You insult me, gentlemen, for not letting me choose. I am no naughty schoolboy. I won't follow a schedule. I will arrange my lessons as I please. To end this squabbling, let's all sit down. *[Bianca to Hortensio]* Play your lute. Cambio's lesson will be finished before you tune your instrument.

HORTENSIO You will end his lesson when my lute is ready?

LUCENTIO That won't happen. Tune your lute. *[HORTENSIO moves away to tune his lute.]*

BIANCA What were you saying?

LUCENTIO Look here, madam. *[LUCENTIO opens a book and reads from it to BIANCA.]* "Here flowed the Simois River in Turkey; here is land near Troy. Here rose the tall palace of the Trojan king Priam.

BIANCA Conster them. 30

LUCENTIO 'Hic ibat,' as I told you before; 'Simois,' I am Lucentio; 'hic est,' son unto Vincentio of Pisa; 'Sigeia tellus,' disguised thus to get your love; 'Hic steterat,' and that Lucentio that comes a-wooing; 'Priami,' is my man Tranio; 'regia,' bearing my port; 'celsa senis,' that we might beguile the old pantaloon. 35

HORTENSIO *[Returning]* Madam, my instrument's in tune.

BIANCA Let's hear.
[HORTENSIO plays.]
O fie, the treble jars!

LUCENTIO Spit in the hole, man, and tune again.
[HORTENSIO returns to tuning his lute.]

BIANCA Now let me see if I can construe it: 'Hic ibat Simois,' I 40
know you not; 'hic est Sigeia tellus,' I trust you not;
'Hic steterat Priami,' take heed he hear us not; 'regia,' presume not; 'celsa senis,' despair not.

HORTENSIO Madam, 'tis now in tune.
[HORTENSIO plays again.]

LUCENTIO All but the bass.

HORTENSIO The bass is right. 'Tis the base knave that jars. 45
[aside] How fiery and forward our pedant is!
Now for my life the knave doth court my love!
Pedascule, I'll watch you better yet.

BIANCA *[To LUCENTIO]* In time I may believe, yet I mistrust.

LUCENTIO Mistrust it not; for sure, Aeacides 50
Was Ajax, call'd so from his grandfather.

BIANCA I must believe my master; else, I promise you,
I should be arguing still upon that doubt.
But let it rest. Now, Litio, to you.
Good master, take it not unkindly, pray, 55
That I have been thus pleasant with you both.

HORTENSIO *[To LUCENTIO]* You may go walk and give me leave
awhile. My lessons make no music in three parts.

BIANCA Explain the lines.

LUCENTIO "Hic ibat" I already translated. "Simois" means "I am Lucentio." "Hic est" means "I am the son of Vincentio of Pisa. "Sigeia tellus" means that I disguised myself as Cambio to win your affection. "Hic steterat" means that I am courting you. "Priami" refers to my servant Tranio. "Regia" means that he pretends to be me. "Celsa senis" means that I want to trick the old fool Hortensio.

HORTENSIO *[HORTENSIO returns]* Madam, my lute is tuned.

BIANCA Let's hear it. *[HORTENSIO strums his lute.]* Oh, shame, the high notes are a-jangle!

LUCENTIO Spit in the center of the lute and try again. *[HORTENSIO tries again to tune his lute.]*

BIANCA Let me see if I can repeat it. "Hic est Sigeia tellus" means "I don't trust you." "Hic steterat Priami" means "Don't let Hortensio hear us." "Regia" means "Don't be too confident. "Celsa senis" means "Don't give up."

HORTENSIO Madam, my lute is in tune. *[HORTENSIO again strums his lute.]*

LUCENTIO All but the bottom notes are in tune.

HORTENSIO The low notes are correct. It's that low rascal Cambio who is out of tune. *[Hortensio to himself]* How impetuous and pushy is this tutor! The felon is flirting with Bianca! Little upstart, I'll keep my eye on you.

BIANCA *[BIANCA to LUCENTIO]* Some day I may trust you, but not yet.

LUCENTIO Don't doubt me. Aeacides was the name that the Greek hero Ajax got from his grandfather Aeacus.

BIANCA I must trust my tutor. Otherwise, I would still quibble over doubt. But forget it. Now, Litio, it's your turn. Good Litio, don't be insulted that I humor you both.

HORTENSIO *[HORTENSIO to LUCENTIO]* Go for a walk and leave me with her. Music lessons don't harmonize three voices.

ACT III

LUCENTIO Are you so formal, sir? *[aside]* Well, I must wait
And watch withal, for, but I be deceiv'd, 60
Our fine musician groweth amorous.
[LUCENTIO moves aside.]

HORTENSIO Madam, before you touch the instrument,
To learn the order of my fingering
I must begin with rudiments of art,
To teach you gamut in a briefer sort, 65
More pleasant, pithy, and effectual
Than hath been taught by any of my trade.
And there it is in writing fairly drawn.

BIANCA Why, I am past my gamut long ago.

HORTENSIO Yet read the gamut of Hortensio. 70
[HORTENSIO hands BIANCA a paper.]

BIANCA *[Reading]* 'Gamut I am, the ground of all accord:
A re, to plead Hortensio's passion;
B mi, Bianca, take him for thy lord,
C fa ut, that loves with all affection;
D sol re, one clef, two notes have I; 75
E la mi, show pity or I die.'
Call you this gamut? Tut, I like it not.
Old fashions please me best. I am not so nice
To change true rules for odd inventions.
[Enter a SERVANT]

SERVANT Mistress, your father prays you leave your books 80
And help to dress your sister's chamber up.
You know tomorrow is the wedding day.

BIANCA Farewell, sweet masters, both. I must be gone.
[Exeunt BIANCA and SERVANT]

LUCENTIO Faith, mistress, then I have no cause to stay.
[Exit]

HORTENSIO But I have cause to pry into this pedant. 85
Methinks he looks as though he were in love.
Yet if thy thoughts, Bianca, be so humble
To cast thy wand'ring eyes on every stale,
Seize thee that list! If once I find thee ranging,
Hortensio will be quit with thee by changing. 90
[Exit]

LUCENTIO Must you be so proper, Hortensio? *[LUCENTIO to himself]* I should wait and keep watch. I am sure this music teacher is romancing Bianca. *[LUCENTIO moves away.]*

HORTENSIO Before you touch the lute and learn to strum it, I must teach you basic music. I will teach you a shortened scale, a pleasant, brief, and useful part of the music trade. Here it is on paper.

BIANCA I learned the scale long ago.

HORTENSIO Read Hortensio's scale. *[HORTENSIO hands BIANCA a paper.]*

BIANCA *[BIANCA reads aloud]* "I am the scale, the basis of harmony. A, a note that declares Hortensio's affection. B, a note that means take me as Bianca's lord. C means that I love you with all my heart. D, I sing two notes. E, either pity me or I will die." Is this your scale? I don't like it. I prefer the original scale. I don't abandon rules for novelties. *[A SERVANT interrupts.]*

SERVANT Miss, your father asks you to stop studying and help decorate Katherina's room. Tomorrow is her wedding day.

BIANCA Goodbye, teachers. I must go. *[BIANCA departs with the SERVANT.]*

LUCENTIO Miss, I have no reason to remain. *[LUCENTIO departs.]*

HORTENSIO I will use this time to investigate this scholar. He acts as though he is infatuated. If you, Bianca, notice every man, any man may have you. If I ever find you flirting, I will give you up for another woman. [HORTENSIO departs.]

ACT III, SCENE 2

The same. Before BAPTISTA'S house.

[Enter BAPTISTA, GREMIO, TRANIO (as Lucentio), KATE, BIANCA, LUCENTIO (as Cambio), and others, ATTENDANTS]

BAPTISTA *[To TRANIO]*
Signior Lucentio, this is the 'pointed day
That Katherina and Petruchio should be married,
And yet we hear not of our son-in-law.
What will be said? What mockery will it be
To want the bridegroom when the priest attends 5
To speak the ceremonial rites of marriage?
What says Lucentio to this shame of ours?

KATE No shame but mine. I must, forsooth, be forc'd
To give my hand, oppos'd against my heart,
Unto a mad-brain rudesby, full of spleen, 10
Who woo'd in haste and means to wed at leisure.
I told you, I, he was a frantic fool,
Hiding his bitter jests in blunt behaviour,
And, to be noted for a merry man,
He'll woo a thousand, 'point the day of marriage, 15
Make feast, invite friends, and proclaim the banns,
Yet never means to wed where he hath woo'd.
Now must the world point at poor Katherina,
And say 'Lo, there is mad Petruchio's wife,
If it would please him come and marry her.' 20

TRANIO Patience, good Katherina, and Baptista too.
Upon my life, Petruchio means but well,
Whatever fortune stays him from his word.
Though he be blunt, I know him passing wise;
Though he be merry, yet withal he's honest. 25

KATE Would Katherina had never seen him though!
[Exit, weeping, followed by BIANCA and others]

BAPTISTA Go, girl, I cannot blame thee now to weep,
For such an injury would vex a very saint;
Much more a shrew of thy impatient humour.
[Enter BIONDELLO]

BIONDELLO Master, master! News! And such old news as you 30
never heard of!

ACT III, SCENE 2

The next day in a street before Baptista's house in Padua in northeastern Italy.

[BAPTISTA enters with GREMIO, TRANIO disguised as Lucentio, KATE, BIANCA, LUCENTIO disguised as Cambio, and other people and servants.]

BAPTISTA *[BAPTISTA to TRANIO]* Lucentio, this is Sunday, the day that Petruchio was going to marry Katherina, but I hear nothing of him. What will people say? How people will laugh when there is no groom to face the priest at the altar. What do you think of my family's shame?

KATE It isn't your shame. It's mine. I must accept a half-witted vulgarian, whom I dislike. He was impulsive to court me hastily. He intends to marry at his own pace. I warned you that he was a crazed fool. He hid his bitter mockery in curt behavior. To earn a reputation as a prankster, he will court a thousand women. He will choose dates, arrange wedding feasts, invite guests, and announce the ceremony. But he has no intention of marrying any of the women he pursues. People will point at poor Katherina. They will say, "Look, there is insane Petruchio's wife, when he decides to come back and marry her."

TRANIO Be patient, Katherina and Baptista. I guarantee that Petruchio has good intentions, whatever keeps him from arriving on time. He is outspoken, but wise. Although he jokes, he is sincere.

KATE I wish I had never seen him! *[KATE departs in tears, followed by BIANCA and others.]*

BAPTISTA Go, Kate. I don't blame you for crying. Such an insult would annoy a saint. A shrew like you would have more reason to be vexed. *[BIONDELLO arrives.]*

BIONDELLO Sir, I have news! Such rare news that you have never heard the like!

BAPTISTA Is it new and old too? How may that be?

BIONDELLO Why, is it not news to hear of Petruchio's coming?

BAPTISTA Is he come?

BIONDELLO Why, no, sir. 35

BAPTISTA What then?

BIONDELLO He is coming.

BAPTISTA When will he be here?

BIONDELLO When he stands where I am and sees you there.

TRANIO But, say, what to thine old news? 40

BIONDELLO Why, Petruchio is coming, in a new hat and an old
Jerkin, a pair of old breeches thrice turned, a pair of boots
that have been candle-cases, one buckled, another laced; an
old rusty sword ta'en out of the town armoury, with a broken
hilt, and chapeless; with two broken points; his 45
horse hipped, with an old mothy saddle and stirrups of no
kindred, besides possessed with the glanders and like to mose
in the chine, troubled with the lampass, infected with the fashions, full of windgalls, sped with spavins, rayed with the yel-
lows, past cure of the fives, stark 50
spoiled with the staggers, begnawn with the bots, swayed in
the back and shoulder-shotten, near-legged before, and with a
half-checked bit and a head-stall of sheep's leather, which,
being restrained to keep him from stumbling, hath been often
burst, and now repaired with knots; one girth 55
six times pieced, and a woman's crupper of velure, which hath
two letters for her name fairly set down in studs, and here and
there pieced with pack-thread.

BAPTISTA Who comes with him?

BIONDELLO O, sir, his lackey, for all the world caparisoned like 60
the horse: with a linen stock on one leg and a kersey boot-
hose on the other, gartered with a red and blue list;
an old hat, and the humour of forty fancies prick'd in't for a
feather. A monster, a very monster in apparel, and not like a
Christian footboy or a gentleman's lackey. 65

TRANIO 'Tis some odd humour pricks him to this fashion,
Yet oftentimes he goes but mean-apparell'd.

BAPTISTA How can you bring news that is old and new?

BIONDELLO The news is that Petruchio's coming.

BAPTISTA Has he arrived?

BIONDELLO Not yet, sir.

BAPTISTA What?

BIONDELLO He is on the way.

BAPTISTA When will he arrive?

BIONDELLO He will get here when you see him standing here.

TRANIO What is the rare news?

BIONDELLO Petruchio is wearing a new hat and an old vest. His pants are thrice repaired. His boots were once candle wrappings. His sword is a rusty relic from the town armory. The hilt is broken; the scabbard has no metal tip. His lacings are frayed on the tips. His horse is lame. The saddle is worn. The stirrups are mismatched. The horse has a swollen throat and watery nose. The mouth is infected and filled with swollen glands. It has lumpy, tumorous legs. It is foul with jaundice and dying of lumps in the ears. Reeling with brain disease gnawed by parasites. Sway-backed and shoulders out of joint. Knock-kneed. The head droops from a half-attached bit and a bridle of sheepskin. To keep him from stumbling, the harness has often split and been tied together. The belly strap has been repaired six times. It bears a tail bridle of velvet suited to a female rider. The length is studded, spelling her initials. The length has been darned with sewing thread.

BAPTISTA Who is coming with Petruchio?

BIONDELLO That is his valet. The man is equipped as poorly as the horse. He wears a linen stocking on one leg and homespun wool hose on the other. His garters are strips of red and blue cloth. He has an old hat adorned with a feather formed of forty pricks. He looks like a monster. He does not resemble a proper footman or a gentleman's valet.

TRANIO Some odd whim causes Petruchio to dress like this. But he is often coarsely dressed.

BAPTISTA I am glad he's come, howsoe'er he comes.

BIONDELLO Why, sir, he comes not.

BAPTISTA Didst thou not say he comes? 70

BIONDELLO Who? That Petruchio came?

BAPTISTA Ay, that Petruchio came.

BIONDELLO No, sir; I say his horse comes with him on his back.

BAPTISTA Why, that's all one.

BIONDELLO *[Sings]* Nay, by Saint Jamy, 75
I hold you a penny,
A horse and a man
Is more than one,
And yet not many.
[Enter PETRUCHIO and GRUMIO]

PETRUCHIO Come, where be these gallants? Who's at home? 80

BAPTISTA You are welcome, sir.

PETRUCHIO And yet I come not well.

BAPTISTA And yet you halt not.

TRANIO Not so well apparell'd
As I wish you were. 85

PETRUCHIO Were it better, I should rush in thus.
But where is Kate? Where is my lovely bride?
How does my father? Gentles, methinks you frown.
And wherefore gaze this goodly company
As if they saw some wondrous monument, 90
Some comet or unusual prodigy?

BAPTISTA Why, sir, you know this is your wedding day.
First were we sad, fearing you would not come,
Now sadder, that you come so unprovided.
Fie, doff this habit, shame to your estate, 95
An eyesore to our solemn festival.

TRANIO And tell us what occasion of import
Hath all so long detain'd you from your wife
And sent you hither so unlike yourself?

BAPTISTA	I'm glad he arrived, however he is dressed.
BIONDELLO	Sir, he isn't coming.
BAPTISTA	I thought you said he was coming.
BIONDELLO	Who? Petruchio?
BAPTISTA	Yes, you said Petruchio was coming.
BIONDELLO	No, sir. I said that his horse is coming with Petruchio on his back.
BAPTISTA	That's the same thing.
BIONDELLO	*[BIONDELLO sings]* By Saint James, I bet you a penny. A man on horseback is more than one, but still not many. *[PETRUCHIO and GRUMIO arrive.]*
PETRUCHIO	Where did all these people come from? Is anyone left at home?
BAPTISTA	Welcome, Petruchio.
PETRUCHIO	I did not arrive well.
BAPTISTA	Aren't you stopping here?
TRANIO	You are poorly dressed.
PETRUCHIO	If I were better dressed, I would hurry. Where is Kate? Where is my beautiful bride? How is my father-in-law? Gentlemen, you are frowning. Why do you gaze at my company as though you saw a comet or some phenomenon?
BAPTISTA	Sir, this is your wedding day. We worried that you would not arrive. Now we worry that you are so ill-prepared. Shame on you. Take off this costume, which disgraces your social status. You are an eyesore at this serious occasion.
TRANIO	What has made you late to your wedding? Why did you arrive in this outrageous dress?

PETRUCHIO Tedious it were to tell, and harsh to hear. 100
Sufficeth, I am come to keep my word,
Though in some part enforced to digress,
Which at more leisure I will so excuse
As you shall well be satisfied withal.
But where is Kate? I stay too long from her. 105
The morning wears. 'Tis time we were at church.

TRANIO See not your bride in these unreverent robes.
Go to my chamber, put on clothes of mine.

PETRUCHIO Not I, believe me. Thus I'll visit her.

BAPTISTA But thus, I trust, you will not marry her. 110

PETRUCHIO Good sooth, even thus. Therefore ha' done with words.
To me she's married, not unto my clothes.
Could I repair what she will wear in me,
As I can change these poor accoutrements,
'Twere well for Kate and better for myself. 115
But what a fool am I to chat with you
When I should bid goodmorrow to my bride
And seal the title with a lovely kiss!
[Exeunt PETRUCHIO and GRUMIO]

TRANIO He hath some meaning in his mad attire.
We will persuade him, be it possible, 120
To put on better ere he go to church.

BAPTISTA I'll after him, and see the event of this.
[Exeunt BAPTISTA, GREMIO, BIONDELLO, and ATTENDANTS]

TRANIO But, sir, to love concerneth us to add
Her father's liking, which to bring to pass,
As I before imparted to your Worship, 125
I am to get a man—whate'er he be
It skills not much, we'll fit him to our turn,—
And he shall be Vincentio of Pisa,
And make assurance here in Padua
Of greater sums than I have promised. 130
So shall you quietly enjoy your hope
And marry sweet Bianca with consent.

PETRUCHIO It's a long, unpleasant story. I arrived as I promised. I was late for a reason I will divulge later. Where is Kate? I have been too long parted from her. It is late morning and time we went to church.

TRANIO Don't escort your bride in these unspeakable garments. Go to my room and dress in my clothes.

PETRUCHIO No. I will receive her as I am.

BAPTISTA But you will not marry her in this attire.

PETRUCHIO Truly, I will. Enough complaining. She's marrying me, not my wardrobe. If I could repair the damage she will do to me as easily as I change clothes, it would be good for Kate and better for me. I am foolish to stand here chatting. I should greet my bride and seal our union with a kiss! *[PETRUCHIO and GRUMIO go out.]*

TRANIO He has a reason for this ridiculous costume. We must convince him to change clothes before he goes to the church.

BAPTISTA I will follow and persuade him. *[BAPTISTA, GREMIO, BIONDELLO, and SERVANTS go out.]*

TRANIO It is my job to gain her father's affection. To succeed, I must find a man—it doesn't matter who plays the part—and claim him as Vincentio of Pisa. And guarantee to Baptista a larger dowry than I promised. If so, you will have Baptista's permission to marry Bianca.

LUCENTIO Were it not that my fellow schoolmaster
Doth watch Bianca's steps so narrowly,
'Twere good, methinks, to steal our marriage, 135
Which, once perform'd, let all the world say no,
I'll keep mine own despite of all the world.

TRANIO That by degrees we mean to look into,
And watch our vantage in this business.
We'll overreach the greybeard, Gremio, 140
The narrowprying father, Minola,
The quaint musician, amorous Litio,
All for my master's sake, Lucentio.
[Enter GREMIO]
Signior Gremio, came you from the church?

GREMIO As willingly as e'er I came from school. 145

TRANIO And is the bride and bridegroom coming home?

GREMIO A bridegroom, say you? 'Tis a groom indeed,
A grumbling groom, and that the girl shall find.

TRANIO Curster than she? Why, 'tis impossible.

GREMIO Why, he's a devil, a devil, a very fiend. 150

TRANIO Why, she's a devil, a devil, the devil's dam.

GREMIO Tut, she's a lamb, a dove, a fool to him.
I'll tell you, Sir Lucentio: when the priest
Should ask if Katherina should be his wife,
'Ay, by gogs-wouns' quoth he, and swore so loud 155
That, all amaz'd, the priest let fall the book,
And as he stoop'd again to take it up,
The mad-brain'd bridegroom took him such a cuff
That down fell priest and book, and book and priest.
'Now take them up,' quoth he 'if any list.' 160

TRANIO What said the wench when he rose again?

LUCENTIO My fellow tutor observes Bianca closely. I should elope with her. Once we are married, whatever the world thinks, I will keep her.

TRANIO I will give that idea some thought and watch for an opportunity. We will outwit the graying Gremio. We will fool the nosy father Minola. We will trick the clever lute player Litio. All to the benefit of Lucentio, my master. *[GREMIO enters.]* Gremio, did you come from the church?

GREMIO As willingly as I left school.

TRANIO Are the bride and groom coming to Baptista's home?

GREMIO A groom? Indeed, he is a grumbly mate for the girl.

TRANIO More ill-tempered than Kate? That's impossible.

GREMIO Petruchio's a demon, a fiend.

TRANIO And she's a demon, Satan's mother.

GREMIO Compared to him, she's a lamb, a dove, a half-wit. I saw it all, Lucentio: When the priest asked if Katherina agreed to be Petruchio's wife, Petruchio yelled, "Yes, by God's wounds," and swore so loud that the startled priest dropped his bible. When he stooped to pick it up, the manic groom struck him so hard that the priest fell on his bible. "Now pick them up," said Petruchio, "if anybody wants to."

TRANIO What did Kate say when the priest got up?

GREMIO Trembled and shook, for why he stamp'd and swore
As if the vicar meant to cozen him.
But after many ceremonies done,
He calls for wine: 'A health!' quoth he, as if 165
He had been aboard, carousing to his mates
After a storm; quaff'd off the muscadel
And threw the sops all in the sexton's face,
Having no other reason
But that his beard grew thin and hungerly, 170
And seem'd to ask him sops as he was drinking.
This done, he took the bride about the neck
And kiss'd her lips with such a clamorous smack
That at the parting all the church did echo.
And I, seeing this, came thence for very shame, 175
And after me I know the rout is coming.
Such a mad marriage never was before!
[Music plays]
Hark, hark! I hear the minstrels play.
[Enter PETRUCHIO, KATE, BIANCA, BAPTISTA, HORTENSIO, GRUMIO, and ATTENDANTS]

PETRUCHIO Gentlemen and friends, I thank you for your pains.
I know you think to dine with me today 180
And have prepar'd great store of wedding cheer,
But so it is, my haste doth call me hence,
And therefore here I mean to take my leave.

BAPTISTA Is't possible you will away to-night?

PETRUCHIO I must away today, before night come. 185
Make it no wonder. If you knew my business,
You would entreat me rather go than stay.
And, honest company, I thank you all,
That have beheld me give away myself
To this most patient, sweet, and virtuous wife. 190
Dine with my father, drink a health to me,
For I must hence, and farewell to you all.

TRANIO Let us entreat you stay till after dinner.

PETRUCHIO It may not be.

GREMIO Let me entreat you. 195

PETRUCHIO It cannot be.

KATE Let me entreat you.

PETRUCHIO I am content.

KATE Are you content to stay?

GREMIO She trembled and quivered because Petruchio stomped and swore that the vicar was trying to cheat him. After the ceremony, Petruchio demanded wine. He called, "A toast!" as if he were a sailor carousing with fellow seamen after a storm. He swallowed the sweet wedding wine and threw the dregs in the caretaker's face. Petruchio gave as his reason that the caretaker's beard was thin and scraggly. The beard seemed to want the dregs of the wine glass. Petruchio grabbed Kate around the neck and kissed her with such a smooch that it echoed through the church. I left out of embarrassment. The rest of the congregation is following me. I've never seen such an improper wedding before! *[Music sounds.]* Listen, the entertainers are playing. *[PETRUCHIO and KATE enter with BIANCA, BAPTISTA, HORTENSIO, GRUMIO, and servants.]*

PETRUCHIO Gentlemen and guests, thanks for coming. I know you intend to join the wedding banquet and share good spirits. But I must hurry away. Therefore, good-bye.

BAPTISTA Are you leaving tonight?

PETRUCHIO I must depart before sundown. You wouldn't be surprised if you knew my errand. You would urge me to hurry on. Thanks to the guests who came to see me wed this obedient, sweet, and pure wife. Dine with my father-in-law, drink a toast to me, for I must hurry away. Good-bye.

TRANIO Please stay until after the banquet.

PETRUCHIO I can't.

GREMIO I beg you.

PETRUCHIO It's impossible.

KATE Let me beg you.

PETRUCHIO That sounds good.

KATE Will you stay for dinner?

PETRUCHIO I am content you shall entreat me stay, 200
But yet not stay, entreat me how you can.

KATE Now, if you love me, stay.

PETRUCHIO Grumio, my horse!

GRUMIO Ay, sir, they be ready; the oats have eaten the horses.

KATE Nay, then, 205
Do what thou canst, I will not go today,
No, nor to-morrow, not till I please myself.
The door is open, sir. There lies your way.
You may be jogging whiles your boots are green.
For me, I'll not be gone till I please myself. 210
'Tis like you'll prove a jolly surly groom,
That take it on you at the first so roundly.

PETRUCHIO O Kate! content thee. Prithee, be not angry.

KATE I will be angry. What hast thou to do?
Father, be quiet. He shall stay my leisure. 215

GREMIO Ay, marry, sir, now it begins to work.

KATE Gentlemen, forward to the bridal dinner.
I see a woman may be made a fool
If she had not a spirit to resist.

PETRUCHIO They shall go forward, Kate, at thy command. 220
Obey the bride, you that attend on her.
Go to the feast, revel and domineer,
Carouse full measure to her maidenhead,
Be mad and merry, or go hang yourselves.
But for my bonny Kate, she must with me. 225
Nay, look not big, nor stamp, nor stare, nor fret;
I will be master of what is mine own.
She is my goods, my chattels; she is my house,
My household stuff, my field, my barn,
My horse, my ox, my ass, my anything. 230
And here she stands, touch her whoever dare.
I'll bring mine action on the proudest he
That stops my way in Padua. Grumio,
Draw forth thy weapon. We are beset with thieves.
Rescue thy mistress, if thou be a man! 235
Fear not, sweet wench, they shall not touch thee, Kate.
I'll buckler thee against a million.
[Exeunt PETRUCHIO, KATE, and GRUMIO]

PETRUCHIO It is good that you beg me. But I won't stay, however much you beg.

KATE If you love me, stay for dinner.

PETRUCHIO Grumio, bring my horse!

GRUMIO It's here, sir. The horses are full of oats.

KATE Whatever you do, I won't leave with you. Nor will I go tomorrow, not until I'm ready. There's the door. There's the road. Trot on while your boots are still new. I won't leave until I choose to. You will be a grumpy groom after behaving so rudely.

PETRUCHIO Kate, be sweet. Please don't be mad.

KATE I will be angry if I want. It is none of your business. Father, say nothing. Petruchio can wait until I am ready to leave.

GREMIO Ah, Baptista, now Petruchio sees the kind of woman he has wed.

KATE Guests, on to the banquet. A woman may be ridiculed if she doesn't fight for herself.

PETRUCHIO The guests will go to the table at the bride's command. Obey the bride, those who side with her. Feast with her, enjoy and have a good time. Carouse to honor her virginity. Be riotous and cheerful, or go to the gallows. But as for my lovely Kate, she will go with me. Don't glare, stomp, gape, or complain. I am master of my wife. She belongs to me. She is like my residence, my goods, my land, my barn, my horse, my ox, my donkey, any property of mine. Don't dare rescue her. I will attack any man who holds me in Padua. Grumio, draw your sword. If you are a man, retrieve your mistress! Don't be afraid, sweet girl, they won't touch you, Kate. I'll fight off a million for you. *[PETRUCHIO, KATE, and GRUMIO depart.]*

BAPTISTA Nay, let them go. A couple of quiet ones!

GREMIO Went they not quickly, I should die with laughing.

TRANIO Of all mad matches, never was the like. 240

LUCENTIO Mistress, what's your opinion of your sister?

BIANCA That, being mad herself, she's madly mated.

GREMIO I warrant him, Petruchio is Kated.

BAPTISTA Neighbours and friends, though bride and bridegroom wants
For to supply the places at the table, 245
You know there wants no junkets at the feast.
Lucentio, you shall supply the bridegroom's place,
And let Bianca take her sister's room.

TRANIO Shall sweet Bianca practise how to bride it?

BAPTISTA She shall, Lucentio. Come, gentlemen, let's go. 250
[Exeunt]

BAPTISTA Let them go. Both are shouters!

GREMIO If they hadn't departed, I would have died laughing.

TRANIO There never was a couple as insanely matched as these.

LUCENTIO Bianca, what is your opinion of Kate?

BIANCA Because she's crazy, she married an insane man.

GREMIO I guarantee that Petruchio is Kated.

BAPTISTA Neighbors and friends, although the bride and groom have left the table, there are no treats lacking from the menu. Lucentio, take the groom's chair. Let Bianca fill Kate's place.

TRANIO Bianca, will you practice being a bride?

BAPTISTA She will, Lucentio. Come, gentlemen, let's dine. *[They all depart for the banquet.]*

ACT IV, SCENE 1

A hall in PETRUCHIO'S country house.

[Enter GRUMIO]

GRUMIO Fie, fie on all tired jades, on all mad masters, and all foul ways! Was ever man so beaten? Was ever man so 'ray'd? Was ever man so weary? I am sent before to make a fire, and they are coming after to warm them. Now, were not I a little pot and soon hot, my very lips might freeze to my 5 teeth, my tongue to the roof of my mouth, my heart in my belly, ere I should come by a fire to thaw me. But I with blowing the fire shall warm myself. For, considering the weather, a taller man than I will take cold. Holla, ho! Curtis! 10
[Enter CURTIS]

CURTIS Who is that calls so coldly?

GRUMIO A piece of ice. If thou doubt it, thou mayst slide from my shoulder to my heel with no greater a run but my head and my neck. A fire, good Curtis.

CURTIS Is my master and his wife coming, Grumio? 15

GRUMIO O, ay, Curtis, ay; and therefore fire, fire! Cast on no water.

CURTIS Is she so hot a shrew as she's reported?

GRUMIO She was, good Curtis, before this frost. But thou knowest winter tames man, woman, and beast, for it hath tamed 20 my old master and my new mistress and myself, fellow Curtis.

CURTIS Away, you three-inch fool! I am no beast.

GRUMIO Am I but three inches? Why, thy horn is a foot, and so long am I, at the least. But wilt thou make a fire? Or shall 25 I complain on thee to our mistress, whose hand—she being now at hand—thus shalt soon feel, to thy cold comfort, for being slow in thy hot office?

CURTIS I prithee, good Grumio, tell me, how goes the world?

GRUMIO A cold world, Curtis, in every office but thine, and 30 therefore fire. Do thy duty, and have thy duty, for my master and mistress are almost frozen to death.

ACT IV, SCENE 1

The greatroom in Petruchio's country house.

[GRUMIO enters.]

GRUMIO Shame on all weary nags, on all raving masters, and on all muddy roads! Has any man ever been so worn down? Has any man ever been so spattered? Has any man ever been so exhausted? Petruchio sent me ahead to build a fire. The newlyweds are coming to warm themselves by the hearth. If I weren't small and quickly warmed, my lips would freeze to my teeth. My tongue would stick to the roof of my mouth, my heart would ice up in my gut, before a fire could thaw me. But I will get warm while blowing on the coals. In this weather, a taller man than I would catch cold. You, Curtis! *[CURTIS enters.]*

CURTIS Who calls me so rudely?

GRUMIO I'm a chunk of ice. You can see for yourself by sliding from my shoulder to my heel. The slope is no faster than from my head to my neck. Build a fire, Curtis.

CURTIS Are my master and his bride coming, Grumio?

GRUMIO Yes, Curtis, they are. So build a fire! Pour on no water.

CURTIS Is she as hot-tempered a scold as her reputation?

GRUMIO She was, Curtis, before today. Cold weather tames man, woman, and animal. It has chilled my master, his wife, and myself, Curtis.

CURTIS Move, you munchkin! I'm not an animal.

GRUMIO Am I a munchkin? Your horns are a foot long. I am at least that long. Are you building the fire? Should I report you to our lady of the house? When she arrives, she will slap you. It will be cold comfort for your failure to build a fire.

CURTIS Tell me, Grumio, how was it in Padua?

GRUMIO Cold in every way, Curtis, so build a fire. Do your job and earn your pay because Petruchio and his wife are freezing.

CURTIS There's fire ready. And therefore, good Grumio, the news?

GRUMIO Why, 'Jack boy, ho, boy!' and as much news as thou wilt. 35

CURTIS Come, you are so full of cony-catching.

GRUMIO Why, therefore fire, for I have caught extreme cold. Where's the cook? Is supper ready, the house trimmed, rushes strewed, cobwebs swept, the servingmen in their 40 new fustian, their white stockings, and every officer his wedding garment on? Be the Jacks fair within, the Jills fair without, the carpets laid, and everything in order?

CURTIS All ready. And therefore, I pray thee, news?

GRUMIO First, know my horse is tired, my master and mistress 45 fallen out.

CURTIS How?

GRUMIO Out of their saddles into the dirt, and thereby hangs a tale.

CURTIS Let's ha't, good Grumio.

GRUMIO Lend thine ear. 45

CURTIS Here.

GRUMIO *[Striking CURTIS]* There.

CURTIS This 'tis to feel a tale, not to hear a tale.

GRUMIO And therefore 'tis called a sensible tale. And this cuff was but to knock at your ear and beseech listening. Now I 50 begin: Imprimis, we came down a foul hill, my master riding behind my mistress—

CURTIS Both of one horse?

GRUMIO What's that to thee?

CURTIS Why, a horse. 55

CURTIS The fire is burning. Well, Grumio, what news do you bring?

GRUMIO I heard a lot of orders, that's all the news I bring.

CURTIS You are quick-witted.

GRUMIO Make the fire quickly. I've caught a bad cold. Where is the cook? Is dinner ready, the house decorated, clean rushes scattered on the floor, cobwebs swept? Are staff members in new cloth and white stockings? Does every servant wear wedding finery? Are the men good-natured and the women pretty? Are the tablecloths spread and everything ready for dinner?

CURTIS Everything is ready. Please, do you bring any news?

GRUMIO Well, my horse is weary, and Petruchio and his bride are quarreling.

CURTIS Why?

GRUMIO They fell off their saddles into the dirt. It's a long story.

CURTIS Tell it, Grumio.

GRUMIO Listen to me.

CURTIS I'm listening.

GRUMIO *[GRUMIO slaps CURTIS.]* There.

CURTIS I feel your story, but I don't hear it.

GRUMIO It's a sensible story. That smack alerts your ear to pay attention. First, we rode down a muddy hill, with Petruchio riding behind his bride—

CURTIS Were both on the same horse?

GRUMIO Why do you care?

CURTIS The horse cares.

GRUMIO Tell thou the tale! But hadst thou not crossed me, thou shouldst have heard how her horse fell, and she under her horse; thou shouldst have heard in how miry a place, how she was bemoiled, how he left her with the horse upon her, how he beat me because her horse stumbled, how she 60 waded through the dirt to pluck him off me, how he swore; how she prayed that never prayed before, how I cried, how the horses ran away, how her bridle was burst, how I lost my crupper; with many things of worthy memory which now shall die in oblivion, and thou return 65 unexperienced to thy grave.

CURTIS By this reck'ning, he is more shrew than she.

GRUMIO Ay; and that thou and the proudest of you all shall find when he comes home. But what talk I of this? Call forth Nathaniel, Joseph, Nicholas, Phillip, Walter, Sugarsop, 70 and the Rest. Let their heads be slickly combed, their blue coats brush'd, and their garters of an indifferent knit. Let them curtsy with their left legs, and not presume to touch a hair of my master's horse-tail till they kiss their hands. Are they all ready? 75

CURTIS They are.

GRUMIO Call them forth.

CURTIS Do you hear, Ho? You must meet my master to countenance my mistress.

GRUMIO Why, she hath a face of her own. 80

CURTIS Who knows not that?

GRUMIO Thou, it seems, that calls for company to countenance her.

CURTIS I call them forth to credit her.

GRUMIO Why, she comes to borrow nothing of them.
[Enter four or five SERVINGMEN]

NATHANIEL Welcome home, Grumio! 85

PHILIP How now, Grumio?

JOSEPH What, Grumio!

NICHOLAS Fellow Grumio!

NATHANIEL How now, old lad?

GRUMIO Then you tell the story! If you hadn't annoyed me, I would have told how her horse fell. She fell under the horse. The place was mucky. She was muddied. He left her under the horse. He beat me because of the accident. She waded through the mire to rescue me. He swore at her. She begged like nobody ever begged before. I wept; the horses ran away. Her bridle broke; I lost the strap under my horse's tail. Because you interrupted, important details are lost. And you must return to your dull job without hearing about it.

CURTIS By your version, he is harsher than she.

GRUMIO You're right. You and the most proper servants will see for yourselves when Petruchio arrives. Why am I talking about all this? Summon Nathaniel, Joseph, Nicholas, Phillip, Walter, Sugarbit, and the rest. Order them to comb their hair, to brush their uniforms, and to wear tasteful garters. Let them bow on their left legs. Let them kiss the couple's hands before grooming the horses. Is everyone ready?

CURTIS They're ready.

GRUMIO Call them in.

CURTIS Do you hear? Come in. You must greet Petruchio and respectfully face his wife.

GRUMIO She has a face of her own.

CURTIS Of course she does!

GRUMIO You asked the staff to face her.

CURTIS I meant to accredit her as lady of the house.

GRUMIO She doesn't need credit to borrow from them. *[Four or five SERVANTS enter.]*

NATHANIEL Welcome home, Grumio!

PHILIP How are you, Grumio?

JOSEPH Hello, Grumio!

NICHOLAS Pal Grumio!

NATHANIEL How are you, old friend?

GRUMIO Welcome, you! How now, you? What, you! Fellow, you! 90
And thus much for greeting. Now, my spruce companions, is all ready, and all things neat?

NATHANIEL All things is ready. How near is our master?

GRUMIO E'en at hand, alighted by this. And therefore be not—
Cock's passion, silence! I hear my master. 95
[Enter PETRUCHIO and KATE]

PETRUCHIO Where be these knaves? What, no man at door
To hold my stirrup nor to take my horse?
Where is Nathaniel, Gregory, Phillip?

ALL SERVANTS Here! Here, sir; here, sir!

PETRUCHIO 'Here, sir! Here, sir! Here, sir! Here, sir!' 100
You loggerheaded and unpolish'd grooms!
What? No attendance? No regard? No duty?
Where is the foolish knave I sent before?

GRUMIO Here, sir, as foolish as I was before.

PETRUCHIO You peasant swain, you whoreson malt-horse drudge! 105
Did I not bid thee meet me in the park
And bring along these rascal knaves with thee?

GRUMIO Nathaniel's coat, sir, was not fully made,
And Gabriel's pumps were all unpink'd i' the heel.
There was no link to colour Peter's hat, 110
And Walter's dagger was not come from sheathing.
There were none fine but Adam, Rafe, and Gregory.
The rest were ragged, old, and beggarly.
Yet, as they are, here are they come to meet you.

GRUMIO Greetings! How are you? Hello! Old pal! That's enough greeting. Now, my neat companions, are you ready? Is everything neat?

NATHANIEL The house is ready. How close is Petruchio?

GRUMIO He is outside and off his horse by now. So don't—God's suffering, hush! I hear Petruchio. *[PETRUCHIO and KATE enter.]*

PETRUCHIO Where are these slackers? Why wasn't there a groom at the door to hold my stirrup and take my horse? Where are Nathaniel, Gregory, Phillip?

ALL SERVANTS Here we are, sir!

PETRUCHIO "Here we are, sir!" You blockheaded and unrefined grooms! What? No one at his post? No respect? No duty to your master? Where is the stupid fool I sent ahead?

GRUMIO Here I am, as stupid as ever.

PETRUCHIO You country lout, you worthless, trudging treadmill horse! Didn't I order you to meet me in the park. And to bring these untrustworthy scoundrels with you?

GRUMIO Nathaniel's coat was not finished, and the heels of Gabriel's shoes weren't decorated with prick marks. There was no charcoal to blacken Peter's hat. And Walter's dagger was being fitted with a sheath. The rest of the staff looked like ragged, aged beggars. They greet you in whatever state you find them.

PETRUCHIO Go, rascals, go, and fetch my supper in. 115
[Exeunt SERVINGMEN]
[Sings] Where is the life that late I led?
Where are those—?
Sit down, Kate, and welcome.
[They sit at the table.]
Food, food, food, food!
[Enter SERVANTS with supper]
Why, when, I say?—Nay, good sweet Kate, be merry. 120
Off with my boots, you rogues! you villains! When?
[Sings] 'It was the friar of orders grey,
As he forth walked on his way'—
[SERVANT begins to remove PETRUCHIO's boots.]
Out, you rogue! You pluck my foot awry. Take that!
[Striking the SERVANT] And mend the plucking off the other. 125
Be merry, Kate. Some water, here! What, ho!
[Enter ONE with water]
Where's my spaniel Troilus? Sirrah, get you hence
And bid my cousin Ferdinand come hither.
[Exit SERVANT]
One, Kate, that you must kiss and be acquainted with.
Where are my slippers? Shall I have some water? 130
Come, Kate, and wash, and welcome heartily.
[SERVANT lets the ewer fall.]
You whoreson villain! Will you let it fall?
[PETRUCHIO strikes him.]

KATE Patience, I pray you, 'twas a fault unwilling.

PETRUCHIO A whoreson, beetle-headed, flap-ear'd knave!
Come, Kate, sit down. I know you have a stomach. 135
Will you give thanks, sweet Kate, or else shall I?
What's this? Mutton?

FIRST SERVANT Ay.

PETRUCHIO Who brought it?

PETER I. 140

PETRUCHIO Go, rascals, and serve my dinner. *[The SERVANTS depart.] [PETRUCHIO sings.]* "Where is my old life? Where are those—?" Sit here, Kate, and welcome to my house. *[The newlyweds sit at the table.]* Bring food, food, food, food! *[SERVANTS arrive with dinner.]* Why are you so slow? Sweet Kate, cheer up. Take off my boots, you louts, you rascals! Now! *[PETRUCHIO sings.]* "A Franciscan monk walks on his way—" *[A SERVANT begins removing PETRUCHIO's boots.]* Go away, you rascal! You twisted my foot. Take that! *[PETRUCHIO slaps the servant.]* Do a better job of pulling off the other boot. Be happy, Kate. Bring water! What's taking so long? *[A SERVANT enters with water.]* Where's my dog Troilus? You, go out and call Cousin Ferdinand. *[The SERVANT exits.]* Kate, you must greet and get to know Ferdinand. Where are my slippers? Are you bringing water? Here, Kate, wash your hands. I heartily welcome you. *[The SERVANT drops the pitcher.]* You worthless lout! Why did you drop it? *[PETRUCHIO hits the servant.]*

KATE Please, Petruchio, it was an accident.

PETRUCHIO A worthless, hammer-headed, flop-eared rascal! Kate, sit down. I know you are hungry. Will you ask the blessing, Kate, or do you want me to? What is this? Mutton?

FIRST SERVANT Yes.

PETRUCHIO Who served it?

PETER I did.

PETRUCHIO 'Tis burnt; and so is all the meat.
What dogs are these? Where is the rascal cook?
How durst you, villains, bring it from the dresser
And serve it thus to me that love it not?
[Throws the meat, etc., at them]
There, take it to you, trenchers, cups, and all! 145
[He throws the food and dishes at them.]
You heedless joltheads and unmanner'd slaves!
What, do you grumble? I'll be with you straight.
[Exeunt SERVANTS]

KATE I pray you, husband, be not so disquiet.
The meat was well, if you were so contented.

PETRUCHIO I tell thee, Kate, 'twas burnt and dried away, 150
And I expressly am forbid to touch it,
For it engenders choler, planteth anger,
And better 'twere that both of us did fast
Since, of ourselves, ourselves are choleric,
Than feed it with such over-roasted flesh. 155
Be patient. Tomorrow 't shall be mended,
And for this night we'll fast for company.
Come, I will bring thee to thy bridal chamber.
[Exeunt PETRUCHIO, KATE, and CURTIS]
[Enter SERVANTS severally]

NATHANIEL Peter, didst ever see the like?

PETER He kills her in her own humour. 160
[Enter CURTIS]

GRUMIO Where is he?

CURTIS In her chamber, making a sermon of continency to her,
And rails and swears and rates, that she, poor soul,
Knows not which way to stand, to look, to speak,
And sits as one new risen from a dream. 165
Away, away, for he is coming hither!
[Exeunt]
[Enter PETRUCHIO]

PETRUCHIO It's burned, like the other meat. Who are these good-for-nothings? Where is the unreliable cook? How dare you, felons, bring me substandard meat from the chopping block? *[PETRUCHIO hurls the mutton and burned meat at the servants.]* There, take it away, platters, cups, and everything! *[PETRUCHIO throws the food and dishes at them.]* You disobedient dunces and discourteous servants! Are you complaining? I'll punish you immediately. *[The SERVANTS go out.]*

KATE Please, husband, don't be so angry. The meat was edible, if you liked it.

PETRUCHIO I insist that it was burned and dried up. I can't eat such food. It causes a hot temper and arouses anger. Both of us should diet since we tend toward anger. We shouldn't eat overcooked meat. Wait until tomorrow, when the cook will do better. Tonight we will eat no meat and enjoy each other's company. Let me escort you to the bridal bedroom. *[PETRUCHIO, KATE, and CURTIS depart.]* *[SERVANTS come in one by one.]*

NATHANIEL Peter, did you ever see such a fuss?

PETER He controls her by mimicking her foul temper. *[CURTIS enters.]*

GRUMIO Where did Petruchio go?

CURTIS He is in her bedroom lecturing her about self-control. He yells, swears, and scolds her to the point that she doesn't know whether to stand, look at him, or speak. She poses like someone awakening from a dream. Let's go. Here comes Petruchio! *[They go out.]* *[PETRUCHIO enters.]*

PETRUCHIO Thus have I politicly begun my reign,
And 'tis my hope to end successfully.
My falcon now is sharp and passing empty.
And till she stoop, she must not be full-gorg'd, 170
For then she never looks upon her lure.
Another way I have to man my haggard,
To make her come and know her keeper's call.
That is, to watch her, as we watch these kites
That bate and beat and will not be obedient. 175
She ate no meat today, nor none shall eat.
Last night she slept not, nor tonight she shall not.
As with the meat, some undeserved fault
I'll find about the making of the bed,
And here I'll fling the pillow, there the bolster, 180
This way the coverlet, another way the sheets.
Ay, and amid this hurly I intend
That all is done in reverend care of her.
And, in conclusion, she shall watch all night,
And, if she chance to nod, I'll rail and brawl, 185
And with the clamour keep her still awake.
This is a way to kill a wife with kindness.
And thus I'll curb her mad and headstrong humour.
He that knows better how to tame a shrew,
Now let him speak; 'tis charity to show. 190
[Exit]

PETRUCHIO I have shrewdly begun my rule over her, and I hope to succeed at taming her. My falcon is hungry. My stomach is empty. Until I tame her, she must not eat. I want her to take the bait. This is the way to tame a female hawk. I will make her obedient to her keeper's call. I will watch her the way a falconer watches hawks that flap their wings in disobedience. She ate nothing today and will get nothing. She didn't sleep last night and won't sleep tonight. As I did with the mutton, I will find fault with the bed linen. I will toss aside the pillow and cushions, the bedspread, and the sheets. I will pretend that this uproar is meant to ensure her comfort. I will keep her awake all night. If she dozes, I will yell and argue and make noise to keep her awake. This is how I will tame a wife with pretended kindness. I will curb her ill temper. If anybody knows a better way to tame a nag like Kate, let him advise me. It would be a kindness to share methods. *[PETRUCHIO goes out.]*

ACT IV, SCENE 2

Padua. Before BAPTISTA'S house.

[Enter TRANIO and HORTENSIO]

TRANIO Is 't possible, friend Litio, that Mistress Bianca
Doth fancy any other but Lucentio?
I tell you, sir, she bears me fair in hand.

HORTENSIO Sir, to satisfy you in what I have said,
Stand by, and mark the manner of his teaching. 5
[They stand aside.]
[Enter BIANCA and LUCENTIO, as Cambio]

LUCENTIO Now mistress, profit you in what you read?

BIANCA What, master, read you? First resolve me that.

LUCENTIO I read that I profess, the *Art to Love.*

BIANCA And may you prove, sir, master of your art!

LUCENTIO While you, sweet dear, prove mistress of my heart. 10
[BIANCA and LUCENTIO move aside, kissing and courting.]

HORTENSIO Quick proceeders, marry! Now tell me, I pray,
You that durst swear that your Mistress Bianca
Lov'd none in the world so well as Lucentio.

TRANIO O despiteful love, unconstant womankind!
I tell thee, Litio, this is wonderful! 15

HORTENSIO Mistake no more. I am not Litio,
Nor a musician as I seem to be,
But one that scorn to live in this disguise
For such a one as leaves a gentleman
And makes a god of such a cullion. 20
Know, sir, that I am call'd Hortensio.

TRANIO Signior Hortensio, I have often heard
Of your entire affection to Bianca,
And since mine eyes are witness of her lightness,
I will with you, if you be so contented, 25
Forswear Bianca and her love forever.

ACT IV, SCENE 2

In a street before Baptista's house in Padua in northeastern Italy.

[Tranio and Hortensio enter.]

TRANIO Is it possible, Litio, that Bianca likes any man but Lucentio? I think she's fond of me.

HORTENSIO To answer your question, I will observe the way that he tutors her in philosophy. *[They stand to one side.]* *[BIANCA enters with LUCENTIO, who is disguised as Cambio.]*

LUCENTIO Miss, are you progressing in your readings?

BIANCA Tell me, what are you reading?

LUCENTIO I read what I practice, Ovid's *Art of Love*.

BIANCA I hope that you master the art!

LUCENTIO You, sweet one, are mistress of my affections. *[BIANCA and LUCENTIO stand aside to kiss and caress each other.]*

HORTENSIO They move directly to lovemaking! Do you still say that Bianca loves no one like she loves Lucentio?

TRANIO Women are spiteful and disloyal! Litio, I am amazed!

HORTENSIO Let me inform you: I am not Litio. I am not a musician. I refuse to remain in disguise. I won't court a woman who abandons a gentleman to adore this loser. Sir, I am Hortensio.

TRANIO Sir, I have heard of your love for Bianca. I have witnessed her waywardness. I agree with you. Let's abandon courting Bianca.

HORTENSIO See, how they kiss and court! Signior Lucentio,
Here is my hand, and here I firmly vow
Never to woo her more, but do forswear her
As one unworthy all the former favours 30
That I have fondly flatter'd her withal.

TRANIO And here I take the like unfeigned oath,
Never to marry with her, though she would entreat.
Fie on her! See how beastly she doth court him!

HORTENSIO Would all the world but he had quite forsworn! 35
For me, that I may surely keep mine oath,
I will be married to a wealthy widow
Ere three days pass, which hath as long lov'd me
As I have lov'd this proud disdainful haggard.
And so farewell, Signior Lucentio. 40
Kindness in women, not their beauteous looks,
Shall win my love, and so I take my leave,
In resolution as I swore before.
[Exit HORTENSIO; LUCENTIO and BIANCA advance.]

TRANIO Mistress Bianca, bless you with such grace
As 'longeth to a lover's blessed case! 45
Nay, I have ta'en you napping, gentle love,
And have forsworn you with Hortensio.

BIANCA Tranio, you jest. But have you both forsworn me?

TRANIO Mistress, we have.

LUCENTIO Then we are rid of Litio. 50

TRANIO I' faith, he'll have a lusty widow now
That shall be woo'd and wedded in a day.

BIANCA God give him joy!

TRANIO Ay, and he'll tame her.

BIANCA He says so, Tranio? 55

TRANIO Faith, he is gone unto the taming-school.

BIANCA The taming-school! What, is there such a place?

TRANIO Ay, mistress, and Petruchio is the master,
That teacheth tricks eleven and twenty long
To tame a shrew and charm her chattering tongue. 60
[Enter BIONDELLO, running]

HORTENSIO Look how they kiss and caress! Lucentio, I offer you my hand and promise never to romance her again. I give up on her. She's unworthy of all the attentions I have showered on her.

TRANIO I will take the same pledge. I would never wed her, even if she begged. Shame on her! See how vulgar she is in enticing him!

HORTENSIO I wish that everyone in the world but Cambio had abandoned her! I plan to keep my promise. Within three days, I plan to marry a rich widow. She loves me as much as I once loved this dismissive baggage. Goodbye, Lucentio. I love women for their kindness, not their beauty. I depart resolved to abandon Bianca. *[HORTENSIO departs. LUCENTIO disguised as Cambio approaches with BIANCA.]*

TRANIO Bianca, I bless you with a true lover's gratitude! I sneaked up on love and denounced it the same way Hortensio did.

BIANCA Tranio, you're joking. Have you and Litio abandoned me?

TRANIO We have, Miss.

LUCENTIO Then we are rid of Litio.

TRANIO He has chosen an energetic widow. He will court and marry her on the same day.

BIANCA I wish them well.

TRANIO And he will tame her.

BIANCA Did he say that, Tranio?

TRANIO He has gone to the taming academy.

BIANCA Taming academy! Is there such a school?

TRANIO Yes, Miss, and Petruchio is the taming master. He teaches winning tricks to humble a nag and to silence her chattering tongue. *[BIONDELLO enters at a run.]*

BIONDELLO O master, master! I have watch'd so long
That I am dog-weary, but at last I spied
An ancient angel coming down the hill
Will serve the turn.

TRANIO What is he, Biondello? 65

BIONDELLO Master, a mercatante or a pedant,
I know not what; but formal in apparel,
In gait and countenance surely like a father.

LUCENTIO And what of him, Tranio?

TRANIO If he be credulous, and trust my tale, 70
I'll make him glad to seem Vincentio
And give assurance to Baptista Minola
As if he were the right Vincentio.
Take in your love, and then let me alone.
[Exeunt LUCENTIO and BIANCA]
[Enter a PEDANT]

PEDANT God save you, sir! 75

TRANIO And you, sir! You are welcome.
Travel you far on, or are you at the farthest?

PEDANT Sir, at the farthest for a week or two,
But then up farther, and as far as Rome,
And so to Tripoli, if God lend me life. 80

TRANIO What countryman, I pray?

PEDANT Of Mantua.

TRANIO Of Mantua, sir? Marry, God forbid!
And come to Padua, careless of your life?

PEDANT My life, sir? How, I pray? For that goes hard. 85

TRANIO 'Tis death for any one in Mantua
To come to Padua. Know you not the cause?
Your ships are stay'd at Venice; and the Duke
For private quarrel 'twixt your duke and him,
Hath publish'd and proclaim'd it openly. 90
'Tis marvel, but that you are but newly come,
You might have heard it else proclaim'd about.

PEDANT Alas, sir, it is worse for me than so,
For I have bills for money by exchange
From Florence, and must here deliver them. 95

BIONDELLO Master, I have kept watch for so long that I am exhausted. I spotted an old fellow coming down the hill who will be useful to us.

TRANIO Who is it, Biondello?

BIONDELLO He's either a peddler or a scholar, I don't know which. He wears formal garments and walks and looks like a father.

LUCENTIO How will you use him, Tranio?

TRANIO If he agrees and trusts my proposition, I will ask him to pose as Vincentio. In the role of Vincentio, he will guarantee to Baptista as Lucentio's father. Take Bianca indoors. Leave this to me. *[LUCENTIO and BIANCA depart.] [A SCHOLAR enters.]*

PEDANT Greetings, sir!

TRANIO And to you, sir! You are welcome here. Are you traveling far or have you reached your destination?

PEDANT I have a week or two of travel left. If I live, I want to go as far south as Rome and on to Tripoli in North Africa.

TRANIO Where are you from?

PEDANT Mantua.

TRANIO From Mantua? Heaven forbid! Do you risk coming east to Padua?

PEDANT Risk my life? Where is there danger? That sounds bad.

TRANIO There is a death sentence in Padua for Mantuans. Didn't you know? Mantuan ships are held in Venice harbor. The Duke of Padua has announced to the public his quarrel with the Duke of Mantua. It is amazing. Since you are new in town, you haven't heard about the grudge match.

PEDANT Sir, I am in a predicament. I have Florentine coins that I must exchange and deliver.

TRANIO Well, sir, to do you courtesy,
This will I do, and this I will advise you.
First tell me, have you ever been at Pisa?

PEDANT Ay, sir, in Pisa have I often been,
Pisa renowned for grave citizens. 100

TRANIO Among them know you one Vincentio?

PEDANT I know him not, but I have heard of him:
A merchant of incomparable wealth.

TRANIO He is my father, sir, and sooth to say,
In countenance somewhat doth resemble you. 105

BIONDELLO *[aside]* As much as an apple doth an oyster, and all one.

TRANIO To save your life in this extremity,
This favour will I do you for his sake
And think it not the worst of all your fortunes
That you are like to Sir Vincentio. 110
His name and credit shall you undertake,
And in my house you shall be friendly lodg'd.
Look that you take upon you as you should.
You understand me, sir. So shall you stay
Till you have done your business in the city. 115
If this be courtesy, sir, accept of it.

PEDANT O sir, I do, and will repute you ever
The patron of my life and liberty.

TRANIO Then go with me, to make the matter good.
This, by the way, I let you understand: 120
My father is here look'd for every day
To pass assurance of a dower in marriage
'Twixt me and one Baptista's daughter here.
In all these circumstances I'll instruct you.
Go with me to clothe you as becomes you. 125
[Exeunt]

TRANIO I will do it for you and give you advice. Have you ever been to Pisa?

PEDANT I have often visited Pisa, where people are polite.

TRANIO Do you know Vincentio?

PEDANT I don't know him, but I've heard of him. He's a very rich merchant.

TRANIO He is my father. He looks very much like you.

BIONDELLO *[BIONDELLO to himself]* He looks as much like Vincentio as an apple resembles an oyster, but no matter.

TRANIO For his sake, I will save your life in Padua. It is lucky that you look like Vincentio. You will pose as Vincentio and stay at my house. You must act the part. You must remain in this role until your business here is done. If you agree, please accept my offer.

PEDANT I do accept and will forever proclaim you my rescuer.

TRANIO Then accompany me. By the way, I must tell you: I expect Vincentio any day now to guarantee a dowry for my marriage to Baptista's daughter. I will fill in the details. Come along so I can provide the proper costume. *[TRANIO and the SCHOLAR depart.]*

ACT IV, SCENE 3

A room in PETRUCHIO'S house.

[Enter KATE and GRUMIO]

GRUMIO No, no, forsooth, I dare not for my life.

KATE The more my wrong, the more his spite appears.
What, did he marry me to famish me?
Beggars that come unto my father's door
Upon entreaty have a present alms. 5
If not, elsewhere they meet with charity.
But I, who never knew how to entreat,
Nor never needed that I should entreat,
Am starv'd for meat, giddy for lack of sleep,
With oaths kept waking, and with brawling fed. 10
And that which spites me more than all these wants,
He does it under name of perfect love,
As who should say, if I should sleep or eat
'Twere deadly sickness, or else present death.
I prithee, go, and get me some repast; 15
I care not what, so it be wholesome food.

GRUMIO What say you to a neat's foot?

KATE 'Tis passing good. I prithee let me have it.

GRUMIO I fear it is too choleric a meat.
How say you to a fat tripe finely broil'd? 20

KATE I like it well. Good Grumio, fetch it me.

GRUMIO I cannot tell. I fear 'tis choleric.
What say you to a piece of beef and mustard?

KATE A dish that I do love to feed upon.

GRUMIO Ay, but the mustard is too hot a little. 25

KATE Why then, the beef, and let the mustard rest.

GRUMIO Nay then, I will not. You shall have the mustard
Or else you get no beef of Grumio.

KATE Then both, or one, or anything thou wilt.

GRUMIO Why then, the mustard without the beef. 30

ACT IV, SCENE 3

A room in Petruchio's country house.

[KATE and GRUMIO enter.]

GRUMIO No, I can't to save my life.

KATE The more he accuses me, the angrier he gets. Did he marry me to starve me? Beggars at Baptista's door get immediate aid. If they don't, they find help somewhere else in Padua. I have never begged or gone hungry. I am starved for food and dizzy from lack of sleep. Petruchio wakes me with shouting and feeds me arguments. He claims to keep me hungry and sleep-deprived out of love for me. He implies that, if I sleep or eat, I will get sick or die immediately. Go, get me food. I don't care what, just so it is edible.

GRUMIO Would you like a calf's foot?

KATE That will do. Bring it here, please.

GRUMIO I am afraid it will arouse your anger. Would you prefer broiled organ meat?

KATE I would. Go get it, Grumio.

GRUMIO I'm not sure about this. I am afraid it will arouse anger in you. What do you think of beef with mustard?

KATE One of my favorite dishes.

GRUMIO The mustard is a bit too hot.

KATE Then bring the beef without the mustard.

GRUMIO No, I won't. You will have mustard or I won't bring beef.

KATE Bring one or both or anything you want.

GRUMIO Then I will bring mustard without beef.

KATE Go, get thee gone, thou false deluding slave,
[Beats him]
That feed'st me with the very name of meat.
Sorrow on thee, and all the pack of you
That triumph thus upon my misery!
Go, get thee gone, I say. 35
[Enter PETRUCHIO and HORTENSIO, with meat]

PETRUCHIO How fares my Kate? What, sweeting, all amort?

HORTENSIO Mistress, what cheer?

KATE Faith, as cold as can be.

PETRUCHIO Pluck up thy spirits. Look cheerfully upon me.
Here, love; thou seest how diligent I am, 40
To dress thy meat myself, and bring it thee.
[Sets the dish on a table]
I am sure, sweet Kate, this kindness merits thanks.
What, not a word? Nay, then thou lov'st it not,
And all my pain is sorted to no proof.
Here, take away this dish. 45

KATE I pray you, let it stand.

PETRUCHIO The poorest service is repaid with thanks,
And so shall mine, before you touch the meat.

KATE I thank you, sir.

HORTENSIO Signior Petruchio, fie! you are to blame. 50
Come, Mistress Kate, I'll bear you company.

PETRUCHIO *[aside]* Eat it up all, Hortensio, if thou lovest me.
Much good do it unto thy gentle heart!
Kate, eat apace. And now, my honey love,
Will we return unto thy father's house 55
And revel it as bravely as the best,
With silken coats and caps and golden rings,
With ruffs and cuffs and farthingales and things,
With scarfs and fans and double change of bravery,
With amber bracelets, beads, and all this knavery. 60
What, hast thou din'd? The tailor stays thy leisure
To deck thy body with his ruffling treasure.
[Enter TAILOR]
Come, tailor, let us see these ornaments.
Lay forth the gown.
[Enter HABERDASHER]
What news with you, sir? 65

KATE Go away, you lying trickster. *[KATE beats GRUMIO.]* You are feeding me only words on a menu. Curses on you and on the whole pack of servants who are enjoying my pain! Go; out, I say. *[PETRUCHIO and HORTENSIO enter with meat.]*

PETRUCHIO How is my Kate? Why are you dejected, sweetheart?

HORTENSIO Lady, what is wrong?

KATE My spirits are cold.

PETRUCHIO Be happy. Look gladly at me. See how attentive I am to cut meat for you and serve it. *[PETRUCHIO sets the dish on the table.]* Certainly I deserve thanks, Kate. You are silent? Then you must not like the meat. My efforts are wasted. Here, take this dish away.

KATE Please, leave it.

PETRUCHIO You thank the worst servant. You must thank me before you eat.

KATE I thank you, sir.

HORTENSIO Petruchio, for shame! It is your fault. Come, Kate. I'll keep you company.

PETRUCHIO *[PETRUCHIO in private to HORTENSIO]* Eat all the meat, Hortensio, if you are my friend. Nourish your good heart! Kate, eat with Hortensio. My sweet love, let's return to Baptista's house. Let us put on an elegant display. We will wear silk coats and caps and gold rings. We will have collars and cuffs and hooped petticoats and things. We will carry scarves and fans and two changes of clothes just for show. We will display amber bracelets, beads, and finery. Have you finished eating? The tailor waits to dress you in ruffles. *[The TAILOR enters.]* Tailor, show us your dressy clothes. Lay out a gown. *[A HAT SELLER enters.]* What fashions do you bring, sir?

HABERDASHER Here is the cap your Worship did bespeak.

PETRUCHIO Why, this was moulded on a porringer!
A velvet dish! Fie, fie, 'tis lewd and filthy.
Why, 'tis a cockle or a walnutshell,
A knack, a toy, a trick, a baby's cap. 70
Away with it! Come, let me have a bigger.

KATE I'll have no bigger. This doth fit the time,
And gentlewomen wear such caps as these.

PETRUCHIO When you are gentle, you shall have one too,
And not till then. 75

HORTENSIO *[aside]* That will not be in haste.

KATE Why, sir, I trust I may have leave to speak,
And speak I will. I am no child, no babe.
Your betters have endur'd me say my mind,
And if you cannot, best you stop your ears. 80
My tongue will tell the anger of my heart,
Or else my heart, concealing it, will break,
And, rather than it shall, I will be free
Even to the uttermost, as I please, in words.

PETRUCHIO Why, thou say'st true. It is a paltry cap, 85
A custard-coffin, a bauble, a silken pie.
I love thee well in that thou lik'st it not.

KATE Love me, or love me not, I like the cap,
And it I will have, or I will have none.
[Exit HABERDASHER]

PETRUCHIO Thy gown? Why, ay. Come, tailor, let us see't. 90
O mercy God, what masquing stuff is here?
What's this? A sleeve? 'Tis like a demi-cannon.
What, up and down carv'd like an apple tart?
Here's snip and nip and cut and slish and slash,
Like to a censer in a barber's shop. 95
Why, what a devil's name, tailor, call'st thou this?

HORTENSIO *[aside]* I see she's like to have neither cap nor gown.

TAILOR You bid me make it orderly and well,
According to the fashion and the time.

HABERDASHER Here is the cap you ordered.

PETRUCHIO This is shaped like a cereal bowl! A velvet bowl! Shame on you, it is trashy and lowly. It's a clamshell or a walnut, a knickknack, a bauble, a joke, a baby's bonnet. Take it away! Bring me something bigger.

KATE I want that size cap. It is in fashion. Gentlewomen prefer this size cap.

PETRUCHIO When you are sweet-natured, you shall have a small cap. But not until then.

HORTENSIO *[HORTENSIO to himself]* That won't happen very soon.

KATE Petruchio, I assume I may speak for myself. And I shall. I am not a child, a baby. People better than you have let me speak for myself. If you can't listen, then stop up your ears. My words will reveal my anger. Or else I will suffer heartbreak from hiding my feelings. Rather than die of heartbreak, I will let my words flow free.

PETRUCHIO You are right. It is a pathetic cap, a pastry shell, a trinket, a cream pie. I love you for rejecting it.

KATE I don't care whether you do or don't love me. I like the cap. I want that one or none. *[The HAT SELLER departs.]*

PETRUCHIO A gown for you? Yes. Come, tailor, show us the gown. God's mercy, what is this costume? Is this a sleeve? It's as big as a cannon. Is it cut like an apple pie? Here's a snip, a nip, a cut, and a slash like a brazier in a barbershop. In the name of Satan, tailor, what style is this?

HORTENSIO *[HORTENSIO to himself]* I think she's not going to get a cap or a gown.

TAILOR You asked me to make it properly and well in the day's fashion.

PETRUCHIO Marry, and did. But if you be remember'd, 100
I did not bid you mar it to the time.
Go, hop me over every kennel home,
For you shall hop without my custom, sir.
I'll none of it. Hence, make your best of it.

KATE I never saw a better fashion'd gown, 105
More quaint, more pleasing, nor more commendable.
Belike you mean to make a puppet of me.

PETRUCHIO Why, true, he means to make a puppet of thee.

TAILOR She says your Worship means to make a puppet of her.

PETRUCHIO O monstrous arrogance! Thou liest, thou thread, 110
Thou thimble,
Thou yard, three-quarters, half-yard, quarter, nail!
Thou flea, thou nit, thou winter-cricket thou!
Brav'd in mine own house with a skein of thread?
Away, thou rag, thou quantity, thou remnant, 115
Or I shall so be-mete thee with thy yard
As thou shalt think on prating whilst thou liv'st!
I tell thee, I, that thou hast marr'd her gown.

TAILOR Your Worship is deceiv'd. The gown is made
Just as my master had direction. 120
Grumio gave order how it should be done.

GRUMIO I gave him no order. I gave him the stuff.

TAILOR But how did you desire it should be made?

GRUMIO Marry, sir, with needle and thread.

TAILOR But did you not request to have it cut? 125

GRUMIO Thou hast faced many things.

TAILOR I have.

GRUMIO Face not me. Thou hast braved many men; brave not me. I will neither be fac'd nor brav'd. I say unto thee, I bid thy master cut out the gown, but I did not bid him cut it to 130
pieces. Ergo, thou liest.

TAILOR Why, here is the note of the fashion to testify.
[He shows the dress order.]

PETRUCHIO Read it.

GRUMIO The note lies in's throat, if he say I said so.

PETRUCHIO Yes, and you did. But, recall, I didn't tell you to ruin it. Shove off to the gutter. I won't patronize you, sir. I refuse the gown. Do what you will with it.

KATE I have never seen so stylish a gown. It is elegant, pleasant, and well made. You are trying to turn me into a puppet.

PETRUCHIO Yes, the tailor wants you to be a puppet.

TAILOR She means that you are making her into a puppet.

PETRUCHIO What arrogance! You are lying. You are a thread, a thimble, a yardstick, three-fourths of a yard, a half yard, a quarter yard, a few inches. You are a flea, a louse egg, an indoor cricket! Insulted in my own house by a length of thread! Out with you, you rag, you length of cloth, you leftover. I will beat you with your yardstick. You will stop to think before retorting, if you survive! You have ruined her gown.

TAILOR You are wrong. I made it just as you asked. Grumio told me what you wanted.

GRUMIO I gave him fabric, but no directions.

TAILOR What kind of gown did you want?

GRUMIO One sewn with needle and thread.

TAILOR Didn't you want me to cut the cloth?

GRUMIO You used trimming.

TAILOR I did.

GRUMIO Don't confront me. You have insulted many customers, but don't insult me. I won't let you confront or insult me. I tell you, I asked you to cut out a gown, but not to cut it to pieces. So, you are lying.

TAILOR Here is the description as proof. *[He holds out the dress order.]*

PETRUCHIO Read it aloud.

GRUMIO The note is a lie if he claims I wrote it.

TAILOR *[Reading]* 'Imprimis, a loose-bodied gown.' 135

GRUMIO Master, if ever I said "loose-bodied gown," sew me in the skirts of it and beat me to death with a bottom of brown thread. I said, 'a gown.'

PETRUCHIO Proceed.

TAILOR 'With a small compassed cape.' 140

GRUMIO I confess the cape.

TAILOR 'With a trunk sleeve.'

GRUMIO I confess two sleeves.

TAILOR 'The sleeves curiously cut.'

PETRUCHIO Ay, there's the villainy. 145

GRUMIO Error i' the bill, sir; error i' the bill! I commanded the sleeves should be cut out and sew'd up again, and that I'll prove upon thee, though thy little finger be armed in a thimble.

TAILOR This is true that I say. An I had thee in place where, thou shouldst know it. 150

GRUMIO I am for thee straight. Take thou the bill, give me thy mete-yard, and spare not me.

HORTENSIO God-a-mercy, Grumio! Then he shall have no odds.

PETRUCHIO Well, sir, in brief, the gown is not for me. 155

GRUMIO You are i' the right, sir, 'tis for my mistress.

PETRUCHIO Go, take it up unto thy master's use.

GRUMIO Villain, not for thy life! Take up my mistress' gown for thy master's use!

PETRUCHIO Why, sir, what's your conceit in that? 160

GRUMIO O, sir, the conceit is deeper than you think for.
Take up my mistress' gown to his master's use!
O, fie, fie, fie!

PETRUCHIO *[aside]* Hortensio, say thou wilt see the tailor paid.
[To TAILOR] Go, take it hence. Be gone, and say no more. 165

TAILOR	[*The TAILOR reads aloud.*] "First, make a loose gown."
GRUMIO	Petruchio, if I said "loose gown," sew me up in the skirts. Beat me to death with a spool of brown thread. I said, "a gown."
PETRUCHIO	Continue.
TAILOR	"With a small, tight cape."
GRUMIO	I did ask for a cape.
TAILOR	"With a full sleeve."
GRUMIO	I asked for two sleeves.
TAILOR	"The sleeve should be creatively cut."
PETRUCHIO	There's the lie.
GRUMIO	The bill is wrong, sir, the bill is wrong! I ordered the sleeves cut out and sewed up. I'll prove my order, even if you arm your little finger with a thimble.
TAILOR	I am correct. If I had you in hand, I would beat you.
GRUMIO	I will take your challenge. You take the bill, give me the yardstick, and go to it.
HORTENSIO	God have mercy, Grumio! The tailor will have no chance.
PETRUCHIO	Well, in conclusion, I don't want the gown.
GRUMIO	You are correct. Your wife wanted the gown.
PETRUCHIO	Return it to your employer.
GRUMIO	Rascal, don't dare take my mistress's gown for your employer to wear!
PETRUCHIO	Why are you joking about this?
GRUMIO	The joke is more significant than you realize. You take my mistress's gown for your employer to wear? Oh, shame, shame, shame!
PETRUCHIO	*[PETRUCHIO in secret]* Hortensio, pay the tailor. *[PETRUCHIO to the TAILOR]* Take it away. Go and say no more.

HORTENSIO *[aside to TAILOR]* Tailor, I'll pay thee for thy gown tomorrow.
Take no unkindness of his hasty words.
Away, I say! Commend me to thy master.
[Exit TAILOR]

PETRUCHIO Well, come, my Kate, we will unto your father's,
Even in these honest mean habiliments. 170
Our purses shall be proud, our garments poor,
For 'tis the mind that makes the body rich,
And as the sun breaks through the darkest clouds,
So honour peereth in the meanest habit.
What, is the jay more precious than the lark 175
Because his feathers are more beautiful?
Or is the adder better than the eel
Because his painted skin contents the eye?
O no, good Kate. Neither art thou the worse
For this poor furniture and mean array. 180
If thou account'st it shame, lay it on me,
And therefore frolic! We will hence forthwith
To feast and sport us at thy father's house.
[To GRUMIO] Go, call my men, and let us straight to him,
And bring our horses unto Long-lane end. 185
There will we mount, and thither walk on foot.
Let's see, I think 'tis now some seven o'clock,
And well we may come there by dinnertime.

KATE I dare assure you, sir, 'tis almost two,
And 'twill be suppertime ere you come there. 190

PETRUCHIO It shall be seven ere I go to horse.
Look what I speak, or do, or think to do,
You are still crossing it. Sirs, let't alone.
I will not go today, and ere I do,
It shall be what o'clock I say it is. 195

HORTENSIO Why, so, this gallant will command the sun!
[Exeunt]

HORTENSIO *[HORTENSIO in secret to the tailor]* Tailor, I will pay you tomorrow for the gown. Pay no attention to his rash complaint. Go and send my greetings to your employer. *[The TAILOR departs.]*

PETRUCHIO Kate, let's depart to Baptista's house, even in these humble garments. Our wallets will be fat, even if our clothes are poor. The mind is prosperous that enriches the body. Just as sunshine breaks through clouds, honor is apparent in the worst clothing. Is a blue jay more valuable than a skylark because the jay's feathers are prettier? Is a snake more valuable than an eel because the snake has a patterned skin? No, Kate. You are no less worthy in worn garments and unstylish costume. If you are ashamed, blame me. Let's have a good time! We will get to Baptista's house to dine and amuse ourselves. [*PETRUCHIO to GRUMIO*] Summon my men. Let's go immediately to Padua. Bring the horses to the end of Long Lane. We will mount and walk on from there. It is now 7:00 a.m. We may arrive by noon.

KATE I am sure it is almost 2:00 p.m. It will be suppertime before we arrive.

PETRUCHIO I won't mount my horse until 7:00 a.m. You are still contradicting what I say, do, or think. Sirs, forget my order. I won't go today. When I do go, it will be at the time I say.

HORTENSIO This challenger will control the sun! *[They depart.]*

ACT IV, SCENE 4

Padua. Before BAPTISTA'S house.

[Enter TRANIO (as Lucentio) and the PEDANT dressed like VINCENTIO]

TRANIO Sir, this is the house. Please it you that I call?

PEDANT Ay, what else? And but I be deceived,
Signior Baptista may remember me,
Near twenty years ago in Genoa,
Where we were lodgers at the Pegasus. 5

TRANIO 'Tis well. And hold your own in any case
With such austerity as 'longeth to a father.

PEDANT I warrant you.
[Enter BIONDELLO]
But, sir, here comes your boy.
'Twere good he were school'd. 10

TRANIO Fear you not him. Sirrah Biondello,
Now do your duty throughly, I advise you.
Imagine 'twere the right Vincentio.

BIONDELLO Tut! Fear not me.

TRANIO But hast thou done thy errand to Baptista? 15

BIONDELLO I told him that your father was at Venice,
And that you look'd for him this day in Padua.

TRANIO Thou'rt a tall fellow. Hold thee that to drink.
[Gives BIONDELLO money]
[Enter BAPTISTA and LUCENTIO (as Cambio)]
Here comes Baptista. Set your countenance, sir.
Signior Baptista, you are happily met. 20
[To the PEDANT] Sir, this is the gentleman I told you of.
I pray you stand good father to me now.
Give me Bianca for my patrimony.

ACT IV, SCENE 4

In a street before Baptista's house in Padua in northeastern Italy.

[TRANIO disguised as LUCENTIO enters with the SCHOLAR, who is disguised as VINCENTIO.]

TRANIO This is the house, sir. May I knock?

PEDANT Of course. Unless I am wrong, Baptista may remember me. Nearly twenty years ago, we lodged together in Genoa in northwestern Italy at the Pegasus Inn.

TRANIO That's good. Be as serious as Lucentio's father Vincentio.

PEDANT I promise. *[BIONDELLO enters.]*
Here comes your servant. He is well trained.

TRANIO Don't worry about him. Biondello, do as I said. Pretend the scholar is Vincentio.

BIONDELLO Don't worry.

TRANIO Have you completed your errand to Baptista?

BIONDELLO I told him that Lucentio's father went to Venice. And that you expect him today in Padua.

TRANIO You are a fine servant. Take this to buy a drink. *[TRANIO gives BIONDELLO a coin.] [BAPTISTA enters with LUCENTIO disguised as Cambio.]*
Here comes Baptista. Put on a serious expression, sir. Baptista, we are lucky to encounter you.
[TRANIO to the SCHOLAR] Sir, this is the man I told you about. Play the role of my father. Win Bianca in exchange for my inheritance.

PEDANT Soft, son!
Sir, by your leave, having come to Padua 25
To gather in some debts, my son Lucentio
Made me acquainted with a weighty cause
Of love between your daughter and himself.
And, for the good report I hear of you,
And for the love he beareth to your daughter 30
And she to him, to stay him not too long,
I am content, in a good father's care,
To have him match'd. And, if you please to like
No worse than I, upon some agreement
Me shall you find ready and willing 35
With one consent to have her so bestow'd,
For curious I cannot be with you,
Signior Baptista, of whom I hear so well.

BAPTISTA Sir, pardon me in what I have to say.
Your plainness and your shortness please me well. 40
Right true it is your son Lucentio here
Doth love my daughter, and she loveth him,
Or both dissemble deeply their affections.
And therefore, if you say no more than this,
That like a father you will deal with him 45
And pass my daughter a sufficient dower,
The match is made, and all is done.
Your son shall have my daughter with consent.

TRANIO I thank you, sir. Where then do you know best
We be affied and such assurance ta'en 50
As shall with either part's agreement stand?

BAPTISTA Not in my house, Lucentio, for you know
Pitchers have ears, and I have many servants.
Besides, old Gremio is heark'ning still,
And happily we might be interrupted. 55

TRANIO Then at my lodging, an it like you.
There doth my father lie, and there this night
We'll pass the business privately and well.
Send for your daughter by your servant here.
[He winks at LUCENTIO.]
My boy shall fetch the scrivener presently. 60
The worst is this: that at so slender warning
You are like to have a thin and slender pittance.

PEDANT Quiet, son! Sir, I come to Padua to collect some debts. My son Lucentio told me how much he loves your daughter Bianca. I hear good things about you. I don't want to delay Lucentio because of the couple's mutual love. As his father, I agree to the match. If you agree, on a contract, I am ready to consent to the marriage, even though we don't agree on all details. Your reputation is good, Baptista.

BAPTISTA Please, let me speak. I am pleased at your brief, uncomplicated reply. It is true that your son Lucentio loves my daughter Bianca, who also loves him. Or else they both pretend to be affectionate. If there is nothing else to discuss, extend my daughter a dowry from your son's inheritance. The match is made and everything worked out. I consent to let Bianca marry your son.

TRANIO Thank you, sir. Is the agreement complete on both sides?

BAPTISTA Not here, Lucentio. There are eavesdroppers. I have a large staff. My neighbor Gremio is still listening. Perhaps there will be interruptions.

TRANIO Come to my quarters, if you wish. My father is lodging with me. We can complete the contract there in private tonight. Send your servant for Bianca. *[TRANIO winks at LUCENTIO.]* My servant will locate a notary. My problem is this: With so little warning, I have little to offer for dinner.

BAPTISTA It likes me well. Cambio, hie you home,
And bid Bianca make her ready straight.
And, if you will, tell what hath happened: 65
Lucentio's father is arriv'd in Padua,
And how she's like to be Lucentio's wife.
[Exit LUCENTIO]

BIONDELLO I pray the gods she may, with all my heart!

TRANIO Dally not with the gods, but get thee gone.
[Exit BIONDELLO]
Signior Baptista, shall I lead the way? 70
Welcome! One mess is like to be your cheer.
Come, sir; we will better it in Pisa.

BAPTISTA I follow you.
[Exeunt TRANIO, PEDANT, and BAPTISTA]
[Enter LUCENTIO and BIONDELLO]

BIONDELLO Cambio!

LUCENTIO What say'st thou, Biondello? 75

BIONDELLO You saw my master wink and laugh upon you?

LUCENTIO Biondello, what of that?

BIONDELLO Faith, nothing; but has left me here behind to expound
the meaning or moral of his signs and tokens.

LUCENTIO I pray thee, moralize them. 80

BIONDELLO Then thus: Baptista is safe, talking with the
deceiving father of a deceitful son.

LUCENTIO And what of him?

BIONDELLO His daughter is to be brought by you to the supper.

LUCENTIO And then? 85

BIONDELLO The old priest at Saint Luke's church is at your
command at all hours.

LUCENTIO And what of all this?

BIONDELLO I cannot tell, except they are busied about a
counterfeit assurance. Take your assurance of her, cum 90
privilegio ad imprimendum solum. To the church! Take the
priest, clerk, and some sufficient honest witnesses.
If this be not that you look for, I have more to say,
But bid Bianca farewell forever and a day.

BAPTISTA I accept. Cambio, tell Bianca to get ready. Tell her what has happened. Lucentio's father Vincentio has arrived in Padua. She may soon be Lucentio's wife. *[LUCENTIO disguised as Cambio departs.]*

BIONDELLO I pray to God she marries Lucentio.

TRANIO Don't dawdle. Go. *[BIONDELLO departs.]* Baptista, follow me. Welcome! You may find only one dish. Come, Baptista. You will have better hospitality in Pisa.

BAPTISTA I'm coming. *[TRANIO departs with the SCHOLAR disguised as Vincentio and with BAPTISTA.] [LUCENTIO and BIONDELLO enter.]*

BIONDELLO Cambio!

LUCENTIO What do you want, Biondello?

BIONDELLO You saw Tranio wink and smile at you?

LUCENTIO So what, Biondello?

BIONDELLO Oh, nothing. He asked me to stay here and explain his meaning.

LUCENTIO Interpret for me, please.

BIONDELLO This is it: Baptista is won over. He confers with a phony father of a fake son.

LUCENTIO What of it?

BIONDELLO His daughter will join you at supper.

LUCENTIO And then?

BIONDELLO The priest at Saint Luke's church awaits you at any time.

LUCENTIO What does this mean?

BIONDELLO I don't know, but the contract they negotiate is phony. To ensure your marriage, use the privilege of betrothal. Hurry to the church! Join the priest, a registrar, and enough witnesses. If this is not what you want, say goodbye to Bianca forever.

LUCENTIO Hear'st thou, Biondello? 95

BIONDELLO I cannot tarry. I knew a wench married in an afternoon as she went to the garden for parsley to stuff a rabbit, and so may you, sir. And so adieu, sir. My master hath appointed me to go to Saint Luke's to bid the priest be ready to come against you come with your appendix. 100
[Exit]

LUCENTIO I may, and will, if she be so contented.
She will be pleas'd. Then wherefore should I doubt?
Hap what hap may, I'll roundly go about her.
It shall go hard if 'Cambio' go without her.
[Exit]

LUCENTIO Is that what you heard, Biondello?

BIONDELLO I can't waste time. I knew a girl who married one afternoon on the excuse that she was picking parsley to stuff a rabbit. Be as quick as she. God be with you, sir. Tranio has sent me to Saint Luke's church to ask the priest to await you and your bride-to-be. *[BIONDELLO goes out.]*

LUCENTIO I will marry her if she agrees. She will be pleased. Do I have any doubt? Come what may, I'll quickly wed her. Only tough obstacles will keep "Cambio" from marrying her. *[LUCENTIO disguised as Cambio departs.]*

ACT IV, SCENE 5

A public road.

[Enter PETRUCHIO, KATE, HORTENSIO, and SERVANTS]

PETRUCHIO Come on, i' God's name, once more toward our father's.
Good Lord, how bright and goodly shines the moon!

KATE The moon? The sun! It is not moonlight now.

PETRUCHIO I say it is the moon that shines so bright.

KATE I know it is the sun that shines so bright. 5

PETRUCHIO Now, by my mother's son, and that's myself,
It shall be moon, or star, or what I list,
Or e're I journey to your father's house.
[To SERVANTS] Go on, and fetch our horses back again.
Evermore cross'd and cross'd, nothing but cross'd! 10

HORTENSIO *[To KATE]* Say as he says, or we shall never go.

KATE Forward, I pray, since we have come so far,
And be it moon, or sun, or what you please.
And if you please to call it a rush candle,
Henceforth I vow it shall be so for me. 15

PETRUCHIO I say it is the moon.

KATE I know it is the moon.

PETRUCHIO Nay, then you lie. It is the blessed sun.

KATE Then God be bless'd, it is the blessed sun.
But sun it is not when you say it is not, 20
And the moon changes even as your mind.
What you will have it nam'd, even that it is,
And so it shall be so for Katherina.

HORTENSIO Petruchio, go thy ways, the field is won.

ACT IV, SCENE 5

A public highway.

[PETRUCHIO enters with KATE, HORTENSIO, and SERVANTS.]

PETRUCHIO Come on, let's go to Baptista's house. The moon shines so bright!

KATE The moon? It is the sun! There is no moonlight now.

PETRUCHIO I say that the moon is shining.

KATE It is the sun shining.

PETRUCHIO I swear, it will be the moon or star or whatever I say or we won't go to Baptista's house.
[PETRUCHIO to his SERVANTS] Take the horses back home. You constantly contradict and contradict, nothing but contradiction.

HORTENSIO *[HORTENSIO to KATE]* Agree with him or we will never get to Padua.

KATE Let's continue, since we've come this far. Let it be moon or sun or whatever you want. Even if you call it a kitchen candle made of dried rushes dipped in grease. From now on, I will agree with you.

PETRUCHIO I say it is the moon.

KATE I agree It is the moon.

PETRUCHIO Then you lie. It is the sun.

KATE Then, bless God, it is the sun. If you say it is not the sun, then it is not. The moon changes shape just like your mind. Whatever you call it, I will agree.

HORTENSIO Petruchio, march on. You have won.

PETRUCHIO Well, forward, forward! Thus the bowl should run, 25
And not unluckily against the bias.
But, soft! Company is coming here.
[Enter VINCENTIO]
[To VINCENTIO] Good-morrow, gentle mistress, where away?
Tell me, sweet Kate, and tell me truly too,
Hast thou beheld a fresher gentlewoman? 30
Such war of white and red within her cheeks!
What stars do spangle heaven with such beauty
As those two eyes become that heavenly face?
Fair lovely maid, once more good day to thee.
Sweet Kate, embrace her for her beauty's sake. 35

HORTENSIO 'A will make the man mad, to make a woman of him.

KATE Young budding virgin, fair and fresh and sweet,
Whither away, or where is thy abode?
Happy the parents of so fair a child.
Happier the man whom favourable stars 40
Allots thee for his lovely bedfellow.

PETRUCHIO Why, how now, Kate? I hope thou art not mad!
This is a man: old, wrinkled, faded, wither'd,
And not a maiden, as thou sayst he is.

KATE Pardon, old father, my mistaking eyes 45
That have been so bedazzled with the sun
That everything I look on seemeth green.
Now I perceive thou art a reverend father.
Pardon, I pray thee, for my mad mistaking.

PETRUCHIO Do, good old grandsire, and withal make known 50
Which way thou travellest. If along with us,
We shall be joyful of thy company.

VINCENTIO Fair sir, and you my merry mistress,
That with your strange encounter much amaz'd me,
My name is called Vincentio, my dwelling Pisa, 55
And bound I am to Padua, there to visit
A son of mine which long I have not seen.

PETRUCHIO What is his name?

VINCENTIO Lucentio, gentle sir.

PETRUCHIO Let's go on. So the bowling ball should roll. It advances fortunately along the course. Halt! Someone is coming. *[VINCENTIO enters.] [PETRUCHIO to VINCENTIO]* Good morning, madam. Where are you going? Kate, have you ever seen a more tender gentlewoman? Look at the cream and blush on her cheeks! Are there stars in the sky as heavenly as her eyes? Pretty girl, good day to you. Kate, give her a hug for her delightful appearance.

HORTENSIO You will drive the man crazy by treating him like a woman.

KATE Young blossoming maiden, pretty and dewy and sweet, where are you going? Where do you live? Your parents must be pleased at so pretty a child. Luckier is the man who beds you.

PETRUCHIO Kate, are you crazy! This is a man—old, wrinkled, faded, withered, and not a girl, as you say.

KATE Forgive my mistake, father. My eyes are so dazzled by the sun that everything I see seems immature. I see that you are a respectable father. Excuse my crazy mistake.

PETRUCHIO Good sire, tell us where you are traveling. If you join our party, we will have fun.

VINCENTIO Sir, you and your jolly wife confused me with your strange greeting. I am Vincentio of Pisa, and I'm going to Padua. I will visit my son, who has been long parted from me.

PETRUCHIO What is his name?

VINCENTIO Lucentio, sir.

PETRUCHIO Happily met, the happier for thy son. 60
And now by law as well as reverend age,
I may entitle thee my loving father.
The sister to my wife, this gentlewoman,
Thy son by this hath married. Wonder not,
Nor be not griev'd. She is of good esteem, 65
Her dowry wealthy, and of worthy birth;
Beside, so qualified as may beseem
The spouse of any noble gentleman.
Let me embrace with old Vincentio,
And wander we to see thy honest son, 70
Who will of thy arrival be full joyous.

VINCENTIO But is this true, or is it else your pleasure,
Like pleasant travellers, to break a jest
Upon the company you overtake?

HORTENSIO I do assure thee, father, so it is. 75

PETRUCHIO Come, go along and see the truth hereof,
For our first merriment hath made thee jealous.
[Exeunt all but HORTENSIO]

HORTENSIO Well, Petruchio, this has put me in heart.
Have to my widow, and if she be froward,
Then hast thou taught Hortensio to be untoward. 80
[Exit]

PETRUCHIO Fortunately for him, we have met you. Now, by age and marriage, I may call you father. Your son married my wife's sister Bianca. Don't worry or fret. She is reputable, rich, and aristocratic. She would make a good wife for any nobleman. Let me greet Vincentio. Let us journey on to Lucentio, who will be glad to see you.

VINCENTIO Is it your habit to joke with travelers you meet on the way?

HORTENSIO Yes, it is, sir.

PETRUCHIO Travel with us and witness the truth about Lucentio. Our joke has made you suspicious. *[All depart except HORTENSIO.]*

HORTENSIO Well, Petruchio, you have encouraged me. Let the widow beware. If she is aggressive, you have taught me to be more stubborn. *[HORTENSIO goes out.]*

ACT V, SCENE 1

Padua. Before LUCENTIO'S house.

[Enter BIONDELLO, LUCENTIO, and BIANCA; GREMIO is out before]

BIONDELLO Softly and swiftly, sir, for the priest is ready.

LUCENTIO I fly, Biondello. But they may chance to need thee at home. Therefore leave us.
[Exit, with BIANCA]

BIONDELLO Nay, faith, I'll see the church a' your back; and then come back to my master's as soon as I can. 5
[He exits.]

GREMIO I marvel Cambio comes not all this while.
[Enter PETRUCHIO, KATE, VINCENTIO, GRUMIO, and ATTENDANTS]

PETRUCHIO Sir, here's the door. This is Lucentio's house.
My father's bears more toward the market-place.
Thither must I, and here I leave you, sir.

VINCENTIO You shall not choose but drink before you go. 10
I think I shall command your welcome here,
And by all likelihood some cheer is toward.
[Knocks]

GREMIO They're busy within. You were best knock louder.
[PEDANT looks out of the window.]

PEDANT *[as VINCENTIO]* What's he that knocks as he would beat down the gate? 15

VINCENTIO Is Signior Lucentio within, sir?

PEDANT He's within, sir, but not to be spoken withal.

VINCENTIO What if a man bring him a hundred pound or two to make merry withal?

PEDANT Keep your hundred pounds to yourself. He shall need 20 none so long as I live.

PETRUCHIO *[To VINCENTIO]* Nay, I told you your son was well beloved in Padua. Do you hear, sir? To leave frivolous circumstances, I pray you tell Signior Lucentio that his father is come from Pisa and is here at the door to speak 25 with him.

ACT V, SCENE 1

In a street before Lucentio's house in Padua in northeastern Italy.

[BIONDELLO, LUCENTIO, and BIANCA enter. GREMIO stands outside.]

BIONDELLO Go quietly and quickly, sir. The priest is ready for the wedding.

LUCENTIO I am hurrying, Biondello. They may need you at home. Leave us. *[LUCENTIO departs with BIANCA.]*

BIONDELLO No, I'll follow you into the church. I will come back to Tranio as soon as I can. *[BIONDELLO exits.]*

GREMIO I wonder why Cambio hasn't arrived. *[PETRUCHIO and KATE enter with VINCENTIO, GRUMIO, and SERVANTS.]*

PETRUCHIO Here's the door of Lucentio's house. Baptista's home is nearer the market. I will leave you here and go to Baptista's house.

VINCENTIO We must have a drink before you go. I will order some hospitality. We will probably find entertainment. *[VINCENTIO knocks at LUCENTIO's door.]*

GREMIO They are busy inside. Knock louder. *[The SCHOLAR looks out of the window.]*

PEDANT *[The scholar disguised as Vincentio]* Who is knocking so vigorously at the gate?

VINCENTIO Is Lucentio home, sir?

PEDANT He is here, but he's busy.

VINCENTIO What if a guest should bring two hundred dollars to pay for amusement?

PEDANT Keep your two hundred dollars. He won't need it as long as I am alive.

PETRUCHIO *[PETRUCHIO to VINCENTIO]* I told you that people in Padua like Lucentio. Did you hear, sir? Quit your celebrating. Tell Lucentio that his father has arrived from Pisa to speak to him.

PEDANT Thou liest. His father is come from Padua and here looking out at the window.

VINCENTIO Art thou his father?

PEDANT Ay, sir, so his mother says, if I may believe her. 30

PETRUCHIO *[To VINCENTIO]* Why, how now, gentleman! Why, this is flat knavery, to take upon you another man's name.

PEDANT Lay hands on the villain. I believe 'a means to cozen somebody in this city under my countenance.
[Enter BIONDELLO]

BIONDELLO I have seen them in the church together. God send 'em 35 good shipping! But who is here? Mine old master, Vincentio! Now we are undone and brought to nothing.

VINCENTIO *[Seeing BIONDELLO]* Come hither, crack-hemp.

BIONDELLO I hope I may choose, sir.

VINCENTIO Come hither, you rogue. What, have you forgot me? 40

BIONDELLO Forgot you? No, sir! I could not forget you, for I never saw you before in all my life.

VINCENTIO What, you notorious villain! Didst thou never see thy master's father, Vincentio?

BIONDELLO What, my old worshipful old master? Yes, marry, sir. See 45 where he looks out of the window.

VINCENTIO Is't so, indeed?
[He beats BIONDELLO.]

BIONDELLO Help, help, help! Here's a madman will murder me.
[Exit]

PEDANT Help, son! Help, Signior Baptista!
[Exit from the window]

PETRUCHIO Prithee, Kate, let's stand aside and see the end of this 50 controversy.
[They stand aside.]
[Enter PEDANT with SERVANTS, BAPTISTA, TRANIO (disguised as Lucentio)]

TRANIO Sir, what are you that offer to beat my servant?

PEDANT	You are lying. His father has come from Padua and is standing here at the window.
VINCENTIO	You are his father?
PEDANT	Yes, according to Lucentio's mother, if she tells the truth.
PETRUCHIO	*[PETRUCHIO to VINCENTIO]* What is this? It is criminal to steal another man's identity.
PEDANT	Arrest him. I fear he intends to pose as me and cheat someone in Padua. *[BIONDELLO enters.]*
BIONDELLO	I have seen Lucentio and Bianca at the church. God send them smooth sailing! Who is this? My old master Vincentio! He will ruin everything.
VINCENTIO	*[VINCENTIO recognizing BIONDELLO]* Come here, noose bait.
BIONDELLO	*[Seeing BIONDELLO]* I will come if I choose, sir.
VINCENTIO	Come here, rascal. Have you forgotten your master?
BIONDELLO	Forgotten you? No, sir! I couldn't forget you because I've never seen you before.
VINCENTIO	What? You criminal! Have you never seen Vincentio, your master's father?
BIONDELLO	Do you mean my wonderful old master? Yes, sir. He is looking out the window.
VINCENTIO	Is he? Really? *[VINCENTIO beats BIONDELLO.]*
BIONDELLO	Help! This lunatic wants to kill me. *[BIONDELLO runs away.]*
PEDANT	Help, Lucentio! Help, Baptista! *[The SCHOLAR leaves the window.]*
PETRUCHIO	Kate, let's stand outside and watch how this dispute ends. *[PETRUCHIO and KATE stand to the side.] [The SCHOLAR enters with SERVANTS, BAPTISTA, and TRANIO disguised as Lucentio.]*
TRANIO	Sir, how dare you beat my servant!

VINCENTIO What am I, sir? Nay, what are you, sir? O immortal gods! O fine villain! A silken doublet, a velvet hose, a scarlet cloak, and a copatain hat! O, I am undone! I am undone! 55
While I play the good husband at home, my son and my servant spend all at the university.

TRANIO How now, what's the matter?

BAPTISTA What, is the man lunatic?

TRANIO Sir, you seem a sober ancient gentleman by your habit, 60
but your words show you a madman. Why, sir, what 'cerns it you if I wear pearl and gold? I thank my good father, I am able to maintain it.

VINCENTIO Thy father! O villain, he is a sailmaker in Bergamo.

BAPTISTA You mistake, sir, you mistake, sir! Pray, what do you 65
think is his name?

VINCENTIO His name? As if I knew not his name! I have brought him up ever since he was three years old, and his name is Tranio.

PEDANT Away, away, mad ass! His name is Lucentio and he is 70
mine only son, and heir to the lands of me, Signior Vincentio.

VINCENTIO Lucentio? O, he hath murdered his master! Lay hold on him, I charge you, in the Duke's name. O, my son, my son! Tell me, thou villain, where is my son Lucentio? 75

TRANIO Call forth an officer.
[Enter an OFFICER]
Carry this mad knave to the gaol. Father Baptista, I charge you see that he be forthcoming.

VINCENTIO Carry me to the gaol!

GREMIO Stay, officer. He shall not go to prison. 80

BAPTISTA Talk not, Signior Gremio. I say he shall go to prison.

GREMIO Take heed, Signior Baptista, lest you be cony-catched in this business. I dare swear this is the right Vincentio.

PEDANT Swear, if thou darest.

GREMIO Nay, I dare not swear it. 85

TRANIO Then thou wert best say that I am not Lucentio.

GREMIO Yes, I know thee to be Signior Lucentio.

VINCENTIO Who am I? Indeed, who are you? Oh heavens, here is a well-dressed villain! A silk vest, velvet stockings, a scarlet cape, and a high-topped hat! Oh, I am ruined! While I am thrifty in Pisa, Lucentio and Tranio spend my money at the university.

TRANIO What is the cause of this squabble?

BAPTISTA Is this man crazy?

TRANIO Sir, you seem like a proper old man by your clothes, but your words make no sense. Why should you care if I wear pearls and gold? I thank my father for providing it.

VINCENTIO Your father? He makes sails northwest of here in Bergamo.

BAPTISTA You are wrong, sir! What do you think his name is?

VINCENTIO His name? Of course I know his name! I have raised him from age three. His name is Tranio.

PEDANT Go away, you raving fool! His name is Lucentio. He is the only son and heir of me, Vincentio.

VINCENTIO He is Lucentio? He has murdered his master! Arrest him, I demand, under the Duke's authority. Oh, my son! Tell me, felon, where is Lucentio?

TRANIO Call a watch officer. *[An OFFICER of the watch enters.]* Haul this madman to jail. Baptista, I demand that you see him tried before the court.

VINCENTIO Send me to jail!

GREMIO Wait, officer. Don't send him to jail.

BAPTISTA Don't interfere, Gremio. I say lock him up.

GREMIO Be careful, Baptista. You might be bamboozled. I swear that this is the real Vincentio.

PEDANT Swear it, if you dare.

GREMIO No, I can't swear it.

TRANIO You are saying that I am not Lucentio.

GREMIO Yes, you are Lucentio.

BAPTISTA Away with the dotard! To the gaol with him!

VINCENTIO Thus strangers may be haled and abus'd. O monstrous villain! 90

[Enter BIONDELLO, LUCENTIO, and BIANCA]

BIONDELLO O, we are spoiled, and yonder he is! Deny him, forswear him, or else we are all undone.

LUCENTIO *[Kneeling]* Pardon, sweet father.

VINCENTIO Lives my sweet son?

[BIONDELLO, TRANIO, and PEDANT exit as fast as may be.]

BIANCA *[Kneeling]* Pardon, dear father. 95

BAPTISTA How hast thou offended?
Where is Lucentio?

LUCENTIO Here's Lucentio,
Right son to the right Vincentio,
That have by marriage made thy daughter mine 100
While counterfeit supposes blear'd thine eyne.

GREMIO Here's packing, with a witness, to deceive us all!

VINCENTIO Where is that damned villain, Tranio,
That fac'd and brav'd me in this matter so?

BAPTISTA Why, tell me, is not this my Cambio? 105

BIANCA Cambio is chang'd into Lucentio.

LUCENTIO Love wrought these miracles. Bianca's love
Made me exchange my state with Tranio,
While he did bear my countenance in the town,
And happily I have arriv'd at the last 110
Unto the wished haven of my bliss.
What Tranio did, myself enforc'd him to.
Then pardon him, sweet father, for my sake.

VINCENTIO I'll slit the villain's nose that would have sent me to the gaol! 115

BAPTISTA *[To LUCENTIO]* But do you hear, sir? Have you married my daughter without asking my good will?

VINCENTIO Fear not, Baptista; we will content you. Go to! But I will in to be revenged for this villainy.

[Exit]

BAPTISTA Take the senile old fool away. Take him to jail!

VINCENTIO Strangers in Padua are nabbed and falsely accused. You monstrous criminal! *[BIONDELLO enters with LUCENTIO and BIANCA.]*

BIONDELLO We are trapped. There is your father! Ignore him, lie about his identity, or we are ruined.

LUCENTIO *[Lucentio kneels before Vincentio.]* Pardon me, dear father.

VINCENTIO Is my dear son alive? *[BIONDELLO, TRANIO, and the SCHOLAR run away as fast as they can.]*

BIANCA *[BIANCA kneels before BAPTISTA.]* Pardon me, my father.

BAPTISTA Why do you ask pardon? Where is Lucentio?

LUCENTIO Here I am, the real son of the real Vincentio. While fakes tricked you, I married Bianca.

GREMIO This is a plot to deceive us!

VINCENTIO Where is that damned rascal Tranio, who confronted and insulted me just now?

BAPTISTA Isn't this Cambio the tutor?

BIANCA Cambio was really Lucentio.

LUCENTIO Love made this miracle. To win Bianca, I traded identities with Tranio. In Padua, Tranio pretended to be me. I have achieved what I wanted—marriage to Bianca. Tranio did what I ordered. Dear father, pardon Tranio for my sake.

VINCENTIO I will slit Tranio's nose for ordering my imprisonment!

BAPTISTA *[BAPTISTA to LUCENTIO]* Are you listening? Have you married my daughter without my permission?

VINCENTIO Don't worry, Baptista, we will satisfy you. Relax! I will wreak vengeance for this trickery. *[VINCENTIO departs.]*

BAPTISTA And I to sound the depth of this knavery. 120
[Exit]

LUCENTIO Look not pale, Bianca. Thy father will not frown.
[Exeunt LUCENTIO and BIANCA]

GREMIO My cake is dough, but I'll in among the rest,
Out of hope of all but my share of the feast.
[Exit]
[PETRUCHIO and KATE advance.]

KATE Husband, let's follow to see the end of this ado.

PETRUCHIO First kiss me, Kate, and we will. 125

KATE What, in the midst of the street?

PETRUCHIO What, art thou ashamed of me?

KATE No, sir, God forbid, but ashamed to kiss.

PETRUCHIO Why, then, let's home again. *[To GRUMIO]* Come, sirrah, let's away. 130

KATE Nay, I will give thee a kiss. *[She kisses him.]* Now pray thee, love, stay.

PETRUCHIO Is not this well? Come, my sweet Kate.
Better once than never, for never too late.
[Exeunt]

BAPTISTA I will follow Vincentio to get to the bottom of this. *[BAPTISTA departs.]*

LUCENTIO Don't be frightened, Bianca. Your father will approve. *[LUCENTIO departs with BIANCA.]*

GREMIO I lost Bianca. But at least I may join guests at the wedding feast. *[GREMIO departs.] [PETRUCHIO and KATE come forward.]*

KATE Petruchio, let's follow them and see how this muddle ends.

PETRUCHIO First, kiss me, Kate, and we will.

KATE Here in the street?

PETRUCHIO Are you ashamed of me?

KATE Not ashamed of you. I am embarrassed by public kissing.

PETRUCHIO Well, let's go back home. *[PETRUCHIO to GRUMIO]* Come, Grumio. Let's leave Padua.

KATE No, I will kiss you. *[KATE kisses PETRUCHIO.]* Please, dear, let's stay.

PETRUCHIO Isn't this pleasant? Come, dear Kate. Better now than never. It's never too late for obedience. *[They depart.]*

ACT V, SCENE 2

A room in LUCENTIO'S house.

[Enter BAPTISTA, VINCENTIO, GREMIO, the PEDANT, LUCENTIO, and BIANCA, PETRUCHIO, KATE, HORTENSIO and WIDOW; the SERVINGMEN, with TRANIO, BIONDELLO, Grumio, bringing in a banquet]

LUCENTIO At last, though long, our jarring notes agree,
And time it is when raging war is done
To smile at 'scapes and perils overblown.
My fair Bianca, bid my father welcome,
While I with self-same kindness welcome thine. 5
Brother Petruchio, sister Katherina,
And thou, Hortensio, with thy loving widow,
Feast with the best, and welcome to my house.
My banquet is to close our stomachs up
After our great good cheer. Pray you, sit down, 10
For now we sit to chat as well as eat.
[They sit at table.]

PETRUCHIO Nothing but sit and sit, and eat and eat!

BAPTISTA Padua affords this kindness, son Petruchio.

PETRUCHIO Padua affords nothing but what is kind.

HORTENSIO For both our sakes I would that word were true. 15

PETRUCHIO Now, for my life, Hortensio fears his widow!

WIDOW Then never trust me if I be afeard.

PETRUCHIO You are very sensible, and yet you miss my sense:
I mean Hortensio is afeard of you.

WIDOW He that is giddy thinks the world turns round. 20

PETRUCHIO Roundly replied.

KATE Mistress, how mean you that?

WIDOW Thus I conceive by him.

PETRUCHIO Conceives by me? How likes Hortensio that?

HORTENSIO My widow says, thus she conceives her tale. 25

PETRUCHIO Very well mended. Kiss him for that, good widow.

ACT V, SCENE 2

A room in the house of Lucentio at Padua in north central Italy.

[BAPTISTA enters with VINCENTIO, GREMIO, the scholar who posed as VINCENTIO, LUCENTIO, BIANCA, PETRUCHIO, KATE, HORTENSIO with the widow he married. SERVANTS, TRANIO, BIONDELLO, and Grumio serve the banquet.]

LUCENTIO At last, the confusion is settled. Our squabble is replaced by tales of our escapes. Danger has blown over. Bianca, welcome my father Vincentio. I will welcome your father Baptista. Brother-in-law Petruchio, Bianca's sister Katherina, and you, Hortensio with your widow, dine on the best food. Be welcome in my home. The feast will fill our stomachs after the wedding celebration. Please, sit down. We will talk while we eat. *[They sit at LUCENTIO's table.]*

PETRUCHIO Here's nothing but sitting and eating!

BAPTISTA Paduans like this hospitality, son-in-law Petruchio.

PETRUCHIO Paduans are kind.

HORTENSIO I wish that were true.

PETRUCHIO I believe that Hortensio is scaring his widow!

WIDOW I'm not afraid of him.

PETRUCHIO You are wise, but you miss my meaning. I think Hortensio is afraid of you.

WIDOW A dizzy man thinks the world is spinning.

PETRUCHIO A good answer.

KATE Ma'am, what do you mean by that remark?

WIDOW That's how I perceive Petruchio.

PETRUCHIO That's how she understands me? How does Hortensio like that?

HORTENSIO My wife says that's how she means her remark.

PETRUCHIO You explain it well. Kiss him as a reward, widow.

KATE 'He that is giddy thinks the world turns round':
I pray you tell me what you meant by that.

WIDOW Your husband, being troubled with a shrew,
Measures my husband's sorrow by his woe. 30
And now you know my meaning.

KATE A very mean meaning.

WIDOW Right, I mean you.

KATE And I am mean indeed, respecting you.

PETRUCHIO To her, Kate! 35

HORTENSIO To her, widow!

PETRUCHIO A hundred marks, my Kate does put her down.

HORTENSIO That's my office.

PETRUCHIO Spoke like an officer! Ha' to thee, lad.
[Drinks to HORTENSIO]

BAPTISTA How likes Gremio these quick-witted folks? 40

GREMIO Believe me, sir, they butt together well.

BIANCA Head and butt! An hasty-witted body
Would say your head and butt were head and horn.

VINCENTIO Ay, mistress bride, hath that awaken'd you?

BIANCA Ay, but not frighted me. Therefore I'll sleep again. 45

PETRUCHIO Nay, that you shall not. Since you have begun,
Have at you for a bitter jest or two.

BIANCA Am I your bird? I mean to shift my bush,
And then pursue me as you draw your bow.
You are welcome all. 50
[Exeunt BIANCA, and KATE, and WIDOW]

PETRUCHIO She hath prevented me. Here, Signior Tranio,
This bird you aim'd at, though you hit her not.
Therefore a health to all that shot and miss'd.

TRANIO O, sir! Lucentio slipp'd me like his greyhound,
Which runs himself, and catches for his master. 55

PETRUCHIO A good swift simile, but something currish.

TRANIO 'Tis well, sir, that you hunted for yourself.
'Tis thought your deer does hold you at a bay.

KATE	"A dizzy man thinks the world is spinning." Explain it to me.
WIDOW	Petruchio, who is married to a scold, equates Hortensio's troubles with his own. Now you know.
KATE	It's a spiteful statement.
WIDOW	I was insulting you.
KATE	I am furious at you.
PETRUCHIO	Get her, Kate!
HORTENSIO	Get her, wife!
PETRUCHIO	I wager one hundred and thirty-four dollars that Kate wins the fight.
HORTENSIO	That's my job.
PETRUCHIO	Well put, Hortensio! A toast to you, Hortensio. *[PETRUCHIO drinks to HORTENSIO.]*
BAPTISTA	Gremio, do you like these quibbling guests?
GREMIO	Sir, they argue well.
BIANCA	Head and argument! A quick-witted person would say that your head and argument were head and horn.
VINCENTIO	Well, bride, are you joining this squabble?
BIANCA	Yes, but I'm not afraid. That's all I will say.
PETRUCHIO	Don't stop. Since you joined the fray, you must expect a retort or two.
BIANCA	Am I your quarry? I will fly to another perch. You must follow me while you prepare another retort. Welcome to you all. *[BIANCA, KATE, and the WIDOW depart with the women.]*
PETRUCHIO	Bianca got the last word. Tranio, you courted Bianca, but didn't win her. I drink to all who wooed and lost.
TRANIO	Lucentio unleashed me like a greyhound. I pursued the quarry for my master.
PETRUCHIO	A quick, but doggy comparison.
TRANIO	It is good that you did your own courting. People think that Katherina terrifies you.

BAPTISTA O, O, Petruchio! Tranio hits you now.

LUCENTIO I thank thee for that gird, good Tranio. 60

HORTENSIO Confess, confess! Hath he not hit you here?

PETRUCHIO A' has a little gall'd me, I confess.
And as the jest did glance away from me,
'Tis ten to one it maim'd you two outright.

BAPTISTA Now, in good sadness, son Petruchio, 65
I think thou hast the veriest shrew of all.

PETRUCHIO Well, I say no. And therefore, for assurance,
Let's each one send unto his wife,
And he whose wife is most obedient
To come at first when he doth send for her 70
Shall win the wager which we will propose.

HORTENSIO Content. What's the wager?

LUCENTIO Twenty crowns.

PETRUCHIO Twenty crowns?
I'll venture so much of my hawk or hound, 75
But twenty times so much upon my wife.

LUCENTIO A hundred, then.

HORTENSIO Content.

PETRUCHIO A match! 'Tis done.

HORTENSIO Who shall begin? 80

LUCENTIO That will I.
Go, Biondello, bid your mistress come to me.

BIONDELLO I go.
[Exit]

BAPTISTA Son, I'll be your half Bianca comes.

LUCENTIO I'll have no halves. I'll bear it all myself. 85
[Enter BIONDELLO]
How now, what news?

BIONDELLO Sir, my mistress sends you word
That she is busy, and she cannot come.

PETRUCHIO How? "She's busy, and she cannot come!"
Is that an answer? 90

BAPTISTA	Ha, Petruchio! Tranio has insulted you.
LUCENTIO	Thanks for that remark, Tranio.
HORTENSIO	Confess! Isn't Tranio right?
PETRUCHIO	He has annoyed me, I confess. I will bet ten to one that the remark hit Hortensio and Lucentio.
BAPTISTA	It is sad to say, Petruchio, that you married the sassiest wife of all.
PETRUCHIO	You are wrong. To prove my point, let's send for our wives. The wife who is most obedient and arrives first to her husband wins the bet for him.
HORTENSIO	Agreed. What's the wager?
LUCENTIO	Ten dollars.
PETRUCHIO	Only ten dollars? I would wager that much on my hawk or my hunting hound. I wager twenty times that much on Kate.
LUCENTIO	Fifty dollars then.
HORTENSIO	I agree.
PETRUCHIO	I accept the bet.
HORTENSIO	Which husband will go first?
LUCENTIO	I will. Biondello, tell Bianca to come here.
BIONDELLO	I will. *[BIONDELLO goes first.]*
BAPTISTA	I will pay half your wager that Bianca obeys.
LUCENTIO	I don't want your money. I will pay it myself. *[BIONDELLO returns.]* Well, what did she say?
BIONDELLO	Bianca replies that she is busy and can't come.
PETRUCHIO	What? "She is busy and can't come!" Is that an appropriate answer?

GREMIO Ay, and a kind one too.
Pray God, sir, your wife send you not a worse.

PETRUCHIO I hope better.

HORTENSIO Sirrah Biondello, go and entreat my wife
To come to me forthwith. 95
[Exit BIONDELLO]

PETRUCHIO O, ho, entreat her!
Nay, then, she must needs come.

HORTENSIO I am afraid, sir,
Do what you can, yours will not be entreated.
[Enter BIONDELLO]
Now, where's my wife? 100

BIONDELLO She says you have some goodly jest in hand.
She will not come. She bids you come to her.

PETRUCHIO Worse and worse. She will not come! O vile,
Intolerable, not to be endur'd!
Sirrah Grumio, go to your mistress, 105
Say I command her come to me.
[Exit GRUMIO]

HORTENSIO I know her answer.

PETRUCHIO What?

HORTENSIO She will not.

PETRUCHIO The fouler fortune mine, and there an end. 110
[Enter KATE]

BAPTISTA Now, by my holidame, here comes Katherina!

KATE What is your will sir, that you send for me?

PETRUCHIO Where is your sister, and Hortensio's wife?

KATE They sit conferring by the parlour fire.

PETRUCHIO Go, fetch them hither. If they deny to come, 115
Swinge me them soundly forth unto their husbands.
Away, I say, and bring them hither straight.
[Exit KATE]

LUCENTIO Here is a wonder, if you talk of a wonder.

HORTENSIO And so it is. I wonder what it bodes.

GREMIO It was a polite answer. Pray that she never sends you an impolite answer.

PETRUCHIO I expect a better answer from Kate.

HORTENSIO Biondello, tell my wife to come here at once. *[BIONDELLO departs.]*

PETRUCHIO You order her! She must obey you.

HORTENSIO I fear, Petruchio, that, whatever you say, Kate will not obey orders. *[BIONDELLO returns.]*
Where is my wife?

BIONDELLO She says you must be joking. She won't come. She asks you to come to her.

PETRUCHIO This is worse. She won't come! Oh, terrible, intolerable, unbearable! Grumio, go to Kate. Say that I command her to come to me. *[GRUMIO departs.]*

HORTENSIO I know what she will say.

PETRUCHIO What?

HORTENSIO She won't come.

PETRUCHIO Then I lose the bet. *[KATE returns.]*

BAPTISTA I swear by all Christianity, here comes Katherina!

KATE What do you want, sir?

PETRUCHIO Where are Bianca and Hortensio's wife?

KATE They are chatting by the parlor fireplace.

PETRUCHIO Bring them here. If they refuse, whip them and drag them to their husbands. Go and come right back. *[KATE departs.]*

LUCENTIO This is a miracle of miracles.

HORTENSIO Yes, it is. What will happen now?

PETRUCHIO Marry, peace it bodes, and love, and quiet life, 120
An awful rule, and right supremacy,
And, to be short, what not that's sweet and happy.

BAPTISTA Now fair befall thee, good Petruchio!
The wager thou hast won, and I will add
Unto their losses twenty thousand crowns, 125
Another dowry to another daughter,
For she is chang'd as she had never been.

PETRUCHIO Nay, I will win my wager better yet,
And show more sign of her obedience,
Her new-built virtue and obedience. 130
[Enter KATE, BIANCA, and WIDOW]
See where she comes, and brings your froward wives
As prisoners to her womanly persuasion.
Katherina, that cap of yours becomes you not.
Off with that bauble, throw it underfoot.
[KATE pulls off her cap and throws it down.]

WIDOW Lord, let me never have a cause to sigh 135
Till I be brought to such a silly pass!

BIANCA Fie, what a foolish duty call you this?

LUCENTIO I would your duty were as foolish too.
The wisdom of your duty, fair Bianca,
Hath cost me a hundred crowns since supper-time! 140

BIANCA The more fool you for laying on my duty.

PETRUCHIO Katherina, I charge thee tell these headstrong women
What duty they do owe their lords and husbands.

WIDOW Come, come, you're mocking. We will have no telling.

PETRUCHIO Come on, I say, and first begin with her. 145

WIDOW She shall not.

PETRUCHIO I say she shall. And first begin with her.

PETRUCHIO Obedience means household peace, love, and a quiet life. A stern mastery and proper control. Briefly, everything that makes for sweet contentment.

BAPTISTA Good luck to you, Petruchio! I will add to your winnings another ten thousand dollars. It is equal to a dowry for another daughter. Kate has changed into a different woman.

PETRUCHIO I will win even more and prove her obedience and goodness. *[KATE returns with BIANCA and the widow.]* Here she comes with your sassy wives, whom she controls with female persuasion. Katherina, that cap looks terrible on you. Take off that decoration and stamp on it! *[KATE removes her cap and throws it on the floor.]*

WIDOW Lord, never let me reduce myself to such dominance!

BIANCA Shame, Kate. Why do you give in to such trivial displays?

LUCENTIO You should be as controlled as Kate. Your disobedience has cost me fifty dollars since suppertime!

BIANCA You're the fool for betting on my obedience.

PETRUCHIO Kate, tell these unruly wives what they owe to their husbands.

WIDOW Don't ridicule us. We won't be lectured.

PETRUCHIO Speak to the widow first, Kate.

WIDOW I won't have it.

PETRUCHIO She will lecture you first.

KATE Fie, fie! Unknit that threatening unkind brow,
And dart not scornful glances from those eyes
To wound thy lord, thy king, thy governor. 150
It blots thy beauty as frosts do bite the meads,
Confounds thy fame as whirlwinds shake fair buds,
And in no sense is meet or amiable.
A woman mov'd is like a fountain troubled,
Muddy, ill-seeming, thick, bereft of beauty, 155
And while it is so, none so dry or thirsty
Will deign to sip or touch one drop of it.
Thy husband is thy lord, thy life, thy keeper,
Thy head, thy sovereign, one that cares for thee,
And for thy maintenance commits his body 160
To painful labour both by sea and land,
To watch the night in storms, the day in cold,
Whilst thou liest warm at home, secure and safe,
And craves no other tribute at thy hands
But love, fair looks, and true obedience— 165
Too little payment for so great a debt.
Such duty as the subject owes the prince,
Even such a woman oweth to her husband;
And when she is froward, peevish, sullen, sour,
And not obedient to his honest will, 170
What is she but a foul contending rebel
And graceless traitor to her loving lord?
I am asham'd that women are so simple
To offer war where they should kneel for peace,
Or seek for rule, supremacy, and sway 175
When they are bound to serve, love, and obey.
Why are our bodies soft and weak and smooth,
Unapt to toil and trouble in the world,
But that our soft conditions and our hearts
Should well agree with our external parts? 180
Come, come, you froward and unable worms!
My mind hath been as big as one of yours,
My heart as great, my reason haply more,
To bandy word for word and frown for frown;
But now I see our lances are but straws, 185
Our strength as weak, our weakness past compare,
That seeming to be most which we indeed least are.
Then vail your stomachs, for it is no boot,
And place your hands below your husband's foot:
In token of which duty, if he please, 190
My hand is ready; may it do him ease.

KATE Shame on you! Don't frown and glare at Hortensio, your lord and master. Frowning destroys your beauty and ruins your reputation in an unseemly way. An angry woman is like a broken fountain. It produces muddy, undrinkable, water that is thick and ugly. While the fountain is broken, no one will drink from it. Your husband is your master, your life, your protector, your adviser, your ruler, your caretaker. For your sake, he labors on sea and land. He watches for storms in the cold while you are safe and warm at home. He asks no other repayment than love, smiles, and obedience. It's a small reward for so great a job. Women owe to their husbands the same duty as subjects owe their prince. When a wife is sassy, whining, pouty, sour, and disobedient, she becomes a rebel. She is a disgraceful traitor to her lord. I regret that women are so foolish that they revolt when they should kneel in peace. They struggle to rule, conquer, and force when they should serve, love, and obey. Why do we have soft, weak, and smooth bodies unsuited to the world's labor and hardship? Our softness and our compassion should reflect the weakness of our bodies. Come, you sassy and weak worms! I was once as loud and contentious, as argumentative and grim as you. I now believe that our weapons are weak as straws. Our strength is in obedience. Conceal your defiance, which is pointless. Submit to your husband. To prove my willingness, I am ready to comfort him if he asks.

PETRUCHIO Why, there's a wench! Come on, and kiss me, Kate.
[They kiss.]

LUCENTIO Well, go thy ways, old lad, for thou shalt ha't.

VINCENTIO 'Tis a good hearing when children are toward.

LUCENTIO But a harsh hearing when women are froward. 195

PETRUCHIO Come, Kate, we'll to bed.
We three are married, but you two are sped.
[To LUCENTIO] 'Twas I won the wager, though you hit the white,
And being a winner, God give you good night!
[Exeunt PETRUCHIO and KATE]

HORTENSIO Now, go thy ways, thou hast tam'd a curst shrew. 200

LUCENTIO 'Tis a wonder, by your leave, she will be tam'd so.
[Exeunt]

PETRUCHIO Good girl! Come, kiss me, Kate. *[PETRUCHIO and KATE kiss.]*

LUCENTIO You win the bet, Petruchio.

VINCENTIO It is good to hear obedient offspring.

LUCENTIO But unpleasant to hear sassy women.

PETRUCHIO Come, Kate, let's go to bed. We three men are husbands, but you two are lost.
[PETRUCHIO to LUCENTIO]
Though you won Bianca, I won the wager. And the winner says, good night to you all. *[PETRUCHIO and KATE depart.]*

HORTENSIO Good for you. You have tamed a loud-mouth nag.

LUCENTIO It is a marvel how he tamed Kate. *[They go out.]*

Questions for Reflection

1. Contrast Gremio, Hortensio, and Lucentio as potential husbands for Baptista's younger daughter. After losing Bianca to Lucentio, why does Hortensio arrange so quickly to marry the widow? Which suitor is more influenced by infatuation, by true love, by beauty, by money, or by challenge? How do they contrast Petruchio's overt grab for a rich, lusty wife?

2. List the differences between Kate's life under Baptista and her new life at Petruchio's country house. In what ways has she bettered herself? What has she lost? Which life offers the most opportunity? the most dignity?

3. Cite lines from the play that stress the wisdom of Tranio as a servant and adviser to a young, impressionable university student. What is Tranio's response to love at first sight?

4. Contrast the marriage arrangements of these couples from the play:

   - Christopher Sly/Bartholomew
   - Lucentio/Bianca
   - Hortensio/widow
   - Petruchio/Kate

   Why did Elizabethan audiences enjoy dramatic quibbles over which mate should dominate the other? over which mate tricks the other? over marital vengeance?

5. Describe Biondello's relationships with Tranio, Lucentio, and Vincentio. What type of actor could best play a befuddled, but well meaning servant? How does Biondello redeem himself upon Vincentio's arrival in Padua? on the day of Lucentio's wedding?

6. Discuss the theme of hospitality. Why is Baptista eager to treat wedding guests to a fine meal? How does an unforeseen guest embarrass Tranio? How does Gremio's greed belittle him? What does Grumio demand for the newlyweds? How does Curtis serve his master?

7. Write an extended definition of wit as displayed by Baptista with Petruchio, Petruchio with Kate, Cambio with Bianca, Litio with Bianca, Grumio with servants, and Petruchio with Bianca? How does wit divulge the gradual taming of Kate? Kate's new perspective on marriage? Petruchio's fascination with his bride?

8. Discuss Shakespeare's presentation of inherited wealth. How do Lucentio, Petruchio, and the Minola daughters profit from rich fathers? Why should Tranio, the sailmaker's son from Bergamo, apologize to Vincentio?

9. Why does Shakespeare describe Pisa as a walled city? What is the likelihood that Paduans would arbitrarily murder all arrivals from Mantua?

10. Analyze Grumio's statement, "Nothing comes amiss so money comes withal." Why does Shakespeare extol a fortune hunter like Petruchio? like Gremio?

11. Discuss the manner in which male parents and suitors negotiate for a bride as though she were property or a family asset. Why does Lucentio treat fellow suitors to a drink? Why does Baptista want to complete the contract out of Gremio's sight? Why is a scrivener necessary to the business deal?

12. What are the effects of hunger, filth, and sleeplessness on Kate's willfulness? How does the method resemble behavior modification, brainwashing, animal training, and prison torture?

13. In what ways is Bianca a worthy daughter, sister, student, substitute bride, fiancée, hostess, and wife? Why is she willing to give up her jewelry, clothes, and suitors to a fierce older sister?

14. Predict the strengths and weaknesses of the three marriages. Which husband is most likely to demand dominance? to feel satisfactorily mated? to be truly loved? to make a worthy parent? to profit financially? What strengths may derive from the closeness of sisters and brothers-in-law? from the relationship of sons-in-law with a generous father-in-law?

15. Discuss the value of this play as an Elizabethan satire on aggressive, demanding females. Why does Shakespeare typify stubborn women as ungrateful? unnatural? unhappy? desperate?

16. Make a chart of the prominence of these details in the comedy:

- pearls and gold
- mismatched hose
- mustard alone
- broken harness
- cap
- tuning a lute
- St. Luke's church
- tipping a servant
- tutoring
- eavesdropping
- mud
- fashionable clothes
- Latin translation
- a musical scale
- Mantuans
- Antonio's death
- dying horse
- feuding dukes
- contract
- betting
- swearing in church
- Florentine coins
- choler
- wedding toasts
- a wink
- a made-up murder
- a window
- dropped bible
- fire at the hearth
- parlor
- Ovid's *Art of Love*
- galleys
- tied hands

Which details express jealousy? dominance? discourtesy? affection? duplicity? torment? intellectual curiosity? vengeance? loyalty? crime? social convention? Elizabethan science?

17. Why is marriage important to the aristocratic social order in Shakespeare's day? What does Bianca's secret courtship imply about the needs of a house-bound maiden and future heiress to negotiate for her betrothal to a university student? How does her choice of a husband differ from Kate's acceptance of Petruchio? Baptista's acceptance of Tranio? the widow's acceptance of Hortensio?

18. Explain the theme of illusion versus reality as it applies to the following situations:

- Lucentio and Bianca's seating in place of the bride and groom
- Kate's agreement that the moon is shining
- translation from Latin and Greek books
- Biondello's befuddlement at seeing Tranio in Lucentio's clothing
- Petruchio's journey to Venice to buy wedding finery
- Baptista's admission that Kate is stubborn
- study of the musical scale
- Biondello's search for an impostor father
- negotiation of a phony marriage contract
- Vincentio's fear that Tranio has murdered Lucentio and stolen his identity

Why does Lucentio's appearance in Act V, Scene 2 force him to acknowledge Vincentio and to admit deception? Why is this section of the play known as the resolution?

19. Why are Paduan women educated at home whereas Lucentio has free range of a foreign town and multiple study opportunities? How does Baptista's control of the girl suit the dangers of the era? Why is Vincentio eager to locate his missing son?

20. Compose an extended definition of rebellion as exhibited by Kate and Bianca. Why does Bianca refuse to let two tutors debate the arrangement of her study schedule? Why does Kate slap Petruchio? What is Petruchio's response after Kate refuses to leave the wedding celebration?

21. What is the tone of the line "No profit grows where is no pleasure ta'en"? Why does Tranio insist that Lucentio enjoy his classes without becoming a university grind? How does the line apply to Petruchio's search for a rich bride? to the taming of the shrew? to the implied romance between Petruchio and Kate?

22. Summarize male attitudes toward courtship. Why does Baptista allow Gremio and Lucentio to engage in a bidding war for Kate? How does Gremio reveal his character by pledging all that he owns to Kate?

23. In what ways is comic relief used in Petruchio's courtship and wedding? Why is the church a meaningful setting for buffoonery? How does his wedding contrast with Lucentio's elopement?

24. Justify the marriage of Hortensio to the widow. What arouses his anger at Bianca? Why does their relationship seem one-sided? superficial? unsatisfying? unlikely to prosper?

25. How does Shakespeare contrast male and female values in the following instances?

    - the barkeep's summons to a constable
    - Bartholomew's weeping for Christopher Sly
    - Kate's tears before the wedding
    - Baptista's signing of a marriage contract
    - Bianca's refusal of Lucentio's summons
    - the husbands' inciting of a fight between Kate and the widow
    - Bianca's withdrawal with female guests to the parlor
    - Petruchio's pretense of taking care of Kate's health
    - Baptista's doubling of Kate's dowry

26. Discuss the choice of these names and their implied meanings: Cambio/exchange, Litio/lawsuit, Bianca/white, Kate/cake, Tranio/cross over, Grumio/lump, Gremio/lap, Vincentio/conquering, Biondello/little blonde, and Lucentio/lighting. Propose significant names for the widow, sailmaker, Duke of Mantua, Duke of Padua, scrivener, priests, constable, Christopher Sly's wife, and the lord who tricks Christopher Sly.

27. Explain the significance of these absent characters to the plot:

    - Duke of Mantua
    - Duke of Padua
    - sailmaker at Bergamo
    - Antonio
    - priest at St. Luke's church
    - priest at Kate's wedding
    - vicar
    - scrivener

    Why does Shakespeare use a disproportionate number of males in the comedy? in the induction? in the acting troupe?

28. How do the induction and the last scene of the comedy illustrate marital misalliance? How does Bartholomew dissuade Christopher Sly from bedding his wife after a long separation? Why does Shakespeare end the husbands' bet and Kate's lecture with Petruchio's retreat to bed with his bride?

29. Summarize the importance of hearsay to the plots of the induction and the comedy. What does Christopher Sly learn secondhand about the doctor's diagnosis of lengthy insanity? Why do male characters overstate Kate's reputation for shrewishness? Which characters seem most afraid of her? Why does Grumio trust his master's power over women?

30. Explain how Shakespeare uses lowly people in a drama that includes a lord, a wealthy Pisan merchant, the Duke of Padua, the Duke of Mantua, and two priests. How do cast members like a hunting master, officers, a sailmaker, Biondello, Bartholomew, Curtis, a scrivener, and Petruchio's other house servants contribute to the action? Why does Shakespeare ennoble Clowder, Echo, Merriman, and Bellman?

31. What is Shakespeare's marital history? Why do literary historians contrast Anne Hathaway to Kate?

32. Why would Elizabethan audiences like plays about public drunkenness, arrests, wayward daughters, social class, the war of the sexes, troubled courtships, meddling, pranks and mischief, revenge, confused identify, matrimony, fortune hunting, generous parents, disguises, bets, and happy endings? What current performances echo those themes and motifs?

33. Characterize the role of the trickster by describing the lord's confusion of Christopher Sly and Bartholomew's role as lady of the house. Summarize the effect of Petruchio's brief appearance at his wedding. Why does Grumio believe that his master is wilier than Kate?

34. Considering a female's use of force to gain her wants, why does Kate tie Bianca's hands and threaten her? Why does Kate stop hitting Petruchio? How does Hortensio react to the smashed lute? Why does Shakespeare describe the head in the lute as a man locked in the pillory? How does the widow risk making a scene at the wedding banquet?

35. How does Shakespeare build sympathy for Kate in Padua? during music lessons? on the road to the country house? at the dinner table on her wedding night? in the bridal chamber? during the fitting with a cap and gown? during dinner with Hortensio? on return to Baptista's house? before kissing Petruchio in the street? during the bet? during the lecture to balky wives?

36. Discuss various forms of power over characters. Include these examples:

    - Lucentio's need of Vincentio's guarantee to complete a marriage contract
    - Kate's hunger and sleeplessness
    - the barkeep's threat to have Christopher Sly arrested
    - Petruchio's violence against the priest
    - Grumio's refusal to serve Kate beef with mustard
    - Baptista's house arrest of Bianca
    - the arrest of Vincentio
    - Christopher Sly's fear of a relapse
    - Petruchio's tantrums on his wedding night

    In what way does the last scene empower Kate? Petruchio? Hortensio?

37. How does Shakespeare stress character transformation? Why is Bianca less amenable in private with tutors than in public with her father? How does she alter after confinement and private tutoring? after betrothal to Lucentio? after their marriage? Why is her transformation less obvious than Kate's?

38. How does Shakespeare ennoble players in the lord's comedy? What are the benefits of watching a play?

39. Summarize what Kate learns from her husband. Why does Shakespeare advocate a hierarchy of father over daughter and husband over wife?

Notes

Notes

Notes

Notes

Notes

Notes

Notes